BEE GEES

HOW DEEP IS YOUR LOVE

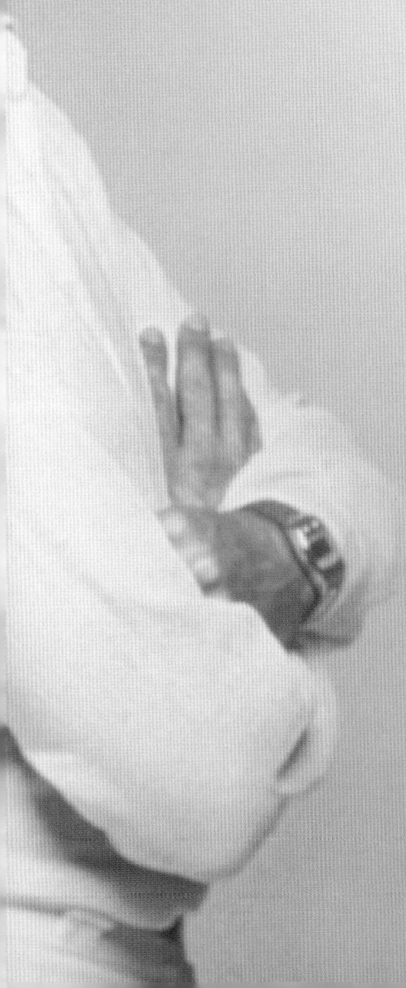

Written By
Michael O'Neill

sona BOOKS

First published in the UK 2021 by Sona Books an imprint of Danann Media Publishing Ltd

CAT NO: SON0482
Photography courtesy of

Getty images:

- Michael Ochs Archives
- Ed Perlstein/Redferns
- GAB Archive/Redferns
- Icon and Image
- Watford/Mirrorpix
- Ivan Keeman/Redferns
- Ron Howard/Redferns
- Keystone-France/Gamma-Keystone
- Monitor Picture Library/Photoshot
- Michael Putland
- Daily Mirror/Mirrorpix
- Express/Archive Photos
- Ed Caraeff
- Koh Hasebe/Shinko Music
- Gijsbert Hanekroot/Redferns
- Jorgen Angel/Redferns
- Richard E. Aaron/Redferns
- Lynn Goldsmith/Corbis/VCG
- Images/Getty Images
- Ed Caraeff
- Richard McCaffrey/ Michael Ochs Archive
- Fin Costello/Redferns
- Luciano Viti
- Brian Rasic
- Ebet Roberts/Redferns
- Stuart Nicol/Evening Standard
- Larry Marano
- Rob Verhorst/Redferns
- Kevin Winter
- Horst Prange/ullstein bild
- Chris Walter/WireImage
- Evening Standard/Hulton Archive

Book layout & design Darren Grice at Ctrl-d
Copy Editor Juliette O'Neill

Made in EU.
ISBN: 978-1-912918-35-5

CONTENTS

INTRODUCTION

From obscurity to megastardom, wealth and glamour, taking in complete musical rejection and a second bout of stardom followed by wrenching personal tragedies, the lives of the brothers Gibb, Barry, Robin, Maurice and Andy, has been a chronicle of the twists and turns, curve balls and golden embraces that life, and especially life as a musician, can bring in its wake.

A family uprooted twice, the Gibbs boys were close-knit brothers who became child stars in Australia and the UK and eventually starting writing songs for such musical luminaries as Barbara Streisand, Dionne Warwick, Dolly Parton and Diana Ross. Their own musical success inspired generations of young musicians following on behind them, and their sound came to define and dominate an entire musical genre in a way no other group had ever done. With Saturday Night Fever, the Bee Gees fired glamour, disco and themselves into the stratosphere, raining glittering costumes, blindingly white smiles and strutting dancers down over the world like whirling confetti. And the world - with the exception of aggravated and jealous rockers - happily went along for the ride.

And what a ride! More than 120 million records sold and the only group in the history of popular music to have written, recorded and produced six consecutive number one hits.

But what of the brothers themselves, inhabiting the red-hot core of this vortex of conflicting emotional highs and lows. Where did the sweetly harmonising kids, gently breathing 'Blowin' in the Wind' out into the world's tv sets from an Australian tv studio, go, once the media latched onto them?

As with so many vulnerable people, the temptation to find a bandaid to paper over the personal fissures that fame can crack wide open did not find them unwilling to play along. Drugs and alcohol were comforting bedfellows when the world seemed too harsh, the reviews too contemptuous, producers appear to pick favourites amongst your siblings, and the gaudy sandcastles in the air came crashing back to earth. Robin and Maurice would battle with the twin demons, as would younger brother Andy, whose addictions were responsible for his early death. Barry managed to steer his course away from trouble to become Sir Barry Gibb in 2018.

Barry alone remains to carry the flame he and his brothers held aloft. The elder brother's trademark falsetto singing indelibly printed the Bee Gees sound onto the consciousness of the listening public, and the music the boys created, their talents and inventiveness, were acknowledged and even admired by many, despite their loud detractors. No less a critic than John Lennon said of them that "they did a damn good job". Praise indeed from an unexpected quarter.

But let's leave the Bee Gees musical legacy in the expert hands of Rolling Stone reviewers: "Is it possible" wrote David Wild, "that we live in a country that can forgive Richard Nixon but not his fellow seventies superstars the Bee Gees.... the Bee Gees are one of the great pop bands of all time".

Enough said.

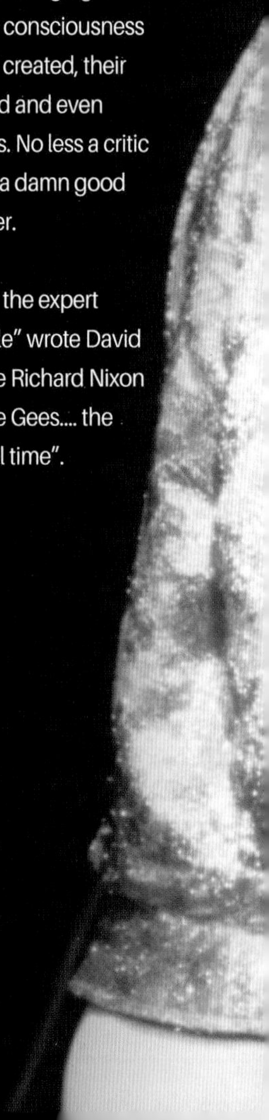

MAIN IMAGE:
The Bee Gees perform at the Oakland Coliseum on July 11, 1979 in Oakland, California

THE ISLE OF WHERE?

Man. The Isle of Man. In the Irish Sea between The Lake District in northern England and Northern Ireland. But I'm getting ahead of myself. The Gibb brothers story actually begins across the water and down the road in Manchester, England, which is just inland and north east of Liverpool. Yes, that Liverpool.

And it was in Manchester that Hugh Gibb began his life in 1916 during World War One. Hugh was destined to be the father of the glamorous harmonic trio. Hugh's love of drums and music had led him to become a band leader by the time the next war was underway, and the Hughie Gibb Orchestra, no less, provided entertainment for the men and women trying to keep the horrors of Nazi warfare and domination from splashing onto Britain's shores.

Hugh was 25 years of age in 1941. He was playing in Manchester, and one of the girls on the dance floor caught his attention. Not one to let such a chance pass by, he flitted over to her and discovered that she, too, had a musical background. She was, in fact, a singer in another local band. War or no war, the harmony between the two continued, and a few months before the WWII ended, baby daughter Lesley Gibb blinked into the light.

Deciding to end their peripatetic lifestyle at last, the Gibbs took up residencies at two hotels on the Isle of Man, where an 18-month-old Lesley was then joined by brother Barry on the 1st of September 1946.

Barry's young years were filled with the sounds of the celebrated crooners and bands of the day, especially Bing Crosby, Hugh's favourite, or Glen Miller, but also, perhaps more significantly for the future career of his little boy, a hugely successful black American quartet that went by the name of the Mills Brothers, "The Four Kings of Harmony". Politeness was their watchword - sensibly in the USA of that era - and broad smiles, two aspects of performance that Hugh would try to get his sons to imitate once they were on their own paths to stardom.

It was a minor miracle that Barry survived childhood at all having pulled a tablecloth and a pot of scalding hot tea down onto himself when he was about 18 months old. Given 20 minutes to live by doctors, he defied the odds, to pull out of a coma and recover. Barry only referred to the incident again in his 70s; "My mother told me I didn't speak for two years, so music and songwriting was my way of escaping my own feelings. I didn't really have any friends"; but his mother felt the incident had given him the strength to be a survivor. After that, his regulated life continued, until one day in December 1949, the 22nd; he was just over three years of age, and his life was about to be changed forever.

Mother Barbara now held twins in her arms; Robin, who had arrived first, and Maurice, whose nickname of Mo would stick with him through into adult life. Robin would remain the quieter of the two, a shy boy, whilst Maurice was an extrovert, keen for attention and approval. But it was Barry - one of the 'triplets' with whom something had gone wrong, as the boys later joked - who assumed responsibility for both of his siblings, a position he would hold for the rest of his brothers' lives. Odd, then, that at school Barry was bullied, donned "Bubbles", and often had to be rescued by big sis Lesley. A time of sadness for the young boy.

Maurice, too, would experience a life-threatening incident in his young years. He fell into the River Dhoo, and only the panicked cries of his son's brothers alerted Hugh to the danger. He rushed into the river behind the house and dragged his son out - thus rescuing disco for the world.

Barry was the first to be seized by music's magnetic pull. Spare time was spent strumming a tennis racquet whilst he sang, or watching entertainers on TV, and he was determined to become a song and dance man following in the soft-shoe-shuffling footsteps of one of his TV idols.

Hugh and Barbara had found it difficult to keep their household going on what they could earn as musicians,

MAIN IMAGE:
Bee Gees portrait, 1963

even when they took on other part time jobs. In 1955, when Barry was nine years old, fate determined that change was in the wind for Hugh Gibb; the Alexandra Hotel did not renew his contract. The family decided to return to the mainland and headed for Manchester. With nowhere to stay, Barry and Hugh went to live with Hugh's father whilst the others took up temporary residence with Barbara's sister. Eventually, they settled at 51 Keppel Road, Chorlton, not far from the town centre and very close to the Old Trafford district.

Manley Park Junior School was now to be the boys' fate, a brisk fifteen-minute walk up the Manchester Road, their short-trousers-clad legs freezing in the icy cold of a Manchester winter. Barry was as unhappy as he had been on the island, except that this time, he chose to avoid trouble by staying out of harms' way. If he didn't go to classes, or even go to school at all, nothing could happen to him; so with Lesley as an ally, the two would not take the bus but simply go back home. As for Robin and Maurice, equally ill-fitted to the life they had been introduced to, they took to setting fire to anything that looked as though it could be turned into flames, drawing the attention and ire of the local constabulary upon themselves. Not an easy time for Hugh and Barbara.

Skipping school meant that Barry had more time for his music passion. Hugh had kindly bought him a simple guitar, and with help from a neighbour and his idol Timmy Steel to inspire him, it didn't take long before his brothers had joined in with Barry's songs and were thrilling themselves by harmonising, producing sounds made more acceptable by the acoustics in their parents' bedroom.

At school, too, the boys would sing whenever and wherever they could, using it as an escape from the lack of integration they experienced, as a way of forming a bastion against the outside world, and one that cemented their closeness. In morning assembly and in choir practice, they gave their all, although a harmonised version of God Save the Queen proved too much for the staid masters of their primary school

When the distant tones of what he assumed was a radio playing music somewhere reached Hugh's ears one day, he was hugely impressed to discover that his own sons were producing the sounds, and from that time on he was determined to help the boys along on a musical path, should they choose it.

Inevitably, their love of harmony fed through to their tastes in popular music, and top of the pops for Maurice at the time were those other harmonising brothers, then at the pinnacle of the industry, the Everly Brothers. The sounds of 'Wake Up Little Susie' would often waft down the stairs to Hugh's ears. But not only; Little Richard and Elvis were also inspiration and joy simultaneously. It was the harmonies, as far as the boys were concerned, that elevated every song.

It was clear that the harmonies were not destined to stay in Hugh's bedroom. By Christmas of 1957 – the Gibbs could never remember the exact date – the decision had been made to go public, and the brothers became 'The Rattlesnakes'; an odd choice for the type of songs they sang and the country they came from. They were going to perform at the Gaumont Theatre cinema between showings of international comedies, when anyone was allowed get up and mime to the favourite singers of the day.

So, bearing their records of The Everly Brothers and Paul Anka, the boys nervously marched off to the Gaumont just after Christmas, Barry in charge of the precious cargo but also wielding his guitar. As they leapt up the theatre steps, disaster. Barry dropped the records. They burst into fragments. Hearts stopped. There was nothing for it they felt. They were primed to perform. They would have to sing live.

Petrified, they walked out onto the stage in front of the 2000-seat auditorium and tried to imagine they were at home in the bedroom. 'Lollipop' by The Mudlarks they knew like their own names, and so off they went.

"The kids" said Maurice many years later, "loved it". The manager was so enthusiastic he asked if they would

MAIN IMAGE:
Bee Gees portrait, 1963

repeat the performance the next week and gave them one shilling each. Riding high as they went back home eager to tell their parents what had happened, Barry was now convinced that they would become famous. No one was doing what they were. The trick would be to make their style outlive the appeal of their youth.

Hugh kept his word and tried to promote the boys, even backing them on drums at another gig at which they earned more than twice the amount they had received at the Gaumont. Soon they were performing more regularly and structuring their songs more methodically. They realised that the name Rattlesnakes had to go, so it did; but finding another wasn't easy, and Wee Johnny Hayes (aka Barry) and the Bluecats wasn't any better.

Just as the lads were taking tentative steps to musical careers, another Gibb was announced to the world, Andy, the last of the tribe, who popped into the Gibb household on March the 5th 1958.

Maintaining this large menagerie had become no easier for Hugh, and periods without work made it far easier to come to the decision that another change was needed to try and keep everything, including his occasionally errant boys, above the water line.

Australia beckoned, offering another chance at reinvention, for the country was looking to expand its population after the war and enticed Brits to move over with the "Ten Pound Pom" plan; ten pounds for a ticket that would normally cost £120. Children could travel gratis. When he announced the emigration plan to the family, no one could quite imagine what life was going to be like. Would they like it? Be homesick? Echoes of Britain were everywhere in place names and the game of cricket; only the weather was better and the sense of expansion, which was still cowering in damp corners in post-war Britain; there was little to lose. So in July 1958, the five-week journey began. Even on the ship, Barry and The Twins sang their hearts out to their fellow Poms and gained a foretaste of a life to come as they enjoyed the time of their lives.

The Gibbs' destination in the new country was Redcliffe to the north-east of Brisbane, Queensland, on Australia's east coast. They'd arrived in paradise. No more northern ice, but swimming in the ocean before school, lizards and banana trees everywhere and a new school; Scarborough State.

For Hugh, a new job as a photographer meant a steady income at last, and the boys went through another reincarnation, this time coming closer to the name the world would know them by, emerging as the Gibb Brothers. As the Gibb Brothers, they entered a talent contest on Brisbane's 4KQ radio station, Talent Quest, for their debut performance in Australia in which they were beaten to first place.

To earn some extra cash, Barry and his friend Ken Griggs had been selling drinks at the Redcliffe Speedway track each Saturday. The track was to prove an important stepping stone for the Bee Gees' careers. Barry had noticed that between races a hiatus opened up when nothing happened, and before long, the enterprising boy and his brothers were singing on a makeshift platform below the grandstand. Which brought them to the attention of the manager of the track, Bill Goode, who was happy for them to keep his crowds entertained in the interval. So, intoxicated by the atmosphere, and standing on board a truck that circumnavigated the track whilst the crowd threw coins towards them in appreciation, the lads warbled their way into the hearts of the crowds – and also manager Bill Goode. He was surprised and mightily impressed by the sounds that emanated from his tannoy system. So impressed, in fact, that the Gibbs received a visit from him shortly afterwards. He wanted to see if these little fellows were the genuine article or not. He inspected their home-made instruments and asked to hear the boys sing. When Barry informed Goode that he could hear one of 180 songs that they had written, the manager was dumbstruck. He'd never heard anything like the boys' singing, and Barry impressed him with his maturity and ability to keep the others on a leash. Even at 12 years of age, Barry knew what he wanted and he could see the potential in their little group.

LEFT:
Bee Gees portrait, 1964

Goode's next move was to get in touch with DJ Bill Gates at 4BH Radio, and he urged him to listen to the boys. His reaction paralleled that of his friend. What do they call themselves, Gates wanted to know. What indeed. Upon discovering they didn't really have a group name, it was Gates who hit upon one; the BG's. From there it was only a short hop to the Bee Gees.

It was far harder to start the boys' music selling. Everyone was on board, especially Hugh, who was struggling to keep the family above the surface.

The Bee Gees recorded six of Barry's songs in the 4BH studio, and Gates pushed the recording until he was blue in the face; his persistence paid off.

TV arrived in Brisbane in 1959, and the Anything Goes programme needed content. The Bee Gees appeared on the show in March 1960 and were a hit, which led to them being offered their own weekly show, the BG's Half Hour. It eventually petered out, but by then they were a known entity and were invited to fill slots on other TV shows. Hugh was doing his bit by finding the lads local gigs in clubs and pubs, which, of course, gave them riotous experiences that no other youngsters of the time were likely to enjoy. Not stardom exactly, but at least standing on the rather rickety rungs of the ladder.

As the 1960s got underway, Barry bid farewell to the educational system that he had long found so restrictive and headed for the real world of work at the age of 15. With as little success as in school. He was saved by his songwriter talent that landed him a 5-year publishing deal at Belinda Music. It was a huge boost in morale, and finances, for everyone.

Family fortunes were further improved by a move to Surfer's Paradise on Australia's Gold Coast, where the Beachcomber Hotel engaged them for an 18-month residency. This led to an audition for the TV show Six O'Clock Rock; slick and confident, the Bee Gees won through to a national TV slot.

MAIN IMAGE:

Bee Gees portrait, 1964

But the breakthrough everyone was longing for was proving hard won. So on the advice of another singer, famous Australia-wide, rock singer-songwriter Col Joye, Hugh, having decided that he would become the Bee Gees' manager full time, uprooted his family one more time and took them off to Sydney. It was 1963 and their house was in Lakemba, West Sydney, where the garden shed became a recording studio.

And all of a sudden, the big time beckoned in the shape of promoter Lee Gordon and his all star shows at the Sydney Stadium, a 100,000-seat venue. Gordon took a chance when the Bee Gees were recommended to him and added them to Chubby Checker's tour that year. Despite the stiff competition, the brothers pulled through and were invited to go to Melbourne and Brisbane as well. Not only that, they bagged a slot on top-rating TV show Bandstand. Not a bad start to the new year.

And then, the news that everyone was craving came through.

Leedon records agreed to make a recording deal with them. It was a brave step, as Barry's song lyrics sat uneasily with the innocence of three teenage boys. And the buying public obviously felt the same, for the first single, about the US civil war, 'The Battle of Blue and Grey', died the death on release and with national DJs, as did the romantic B -side offering. In fact, all the sugar-coated singles they released over the following year melted into nothing. The excitement had melted, too; they had hit the buffers it seemed and the competition was fierce, what with Beatles changing the musical railway points overnight, making even Elvis look like a fossil.

Barry was aware of the seismic shift – how could he not be when the Beatles toured Australia in early 1964 and the country went off its collective trolley for 18 days – and he was longing to break out of the watery wasteland the Bee Gees had waded into. And after their series of failed records, the recording contract was close to being ripped up, too. Only Barry's prolific songwriting talent was saving the day, with one of his many songs, often sung by local stars, reaching No. 2 in NSW in 1964. But the songs were finding their way to international ears, too,

After the Bee Gees went to see the Beatles in Sydney, Barry wanted to become the Beatles. One thing was certain, the boys, too, needed a dramatic change; they, too, needed songs that sounded that fresh and sharp.

They and every other young band in the country.

The Beatles covers they recorded soon after showed they were on the right track, and 'Wine and Women', lyrics by Barry, though still stretching the listener's gullibility, forced its way into one of the three top 20 charts in Sydney – with a little help from their own A$400. Lesley's Bee Gees fan club did their part, too, targeting the important stores, armed with dollars.

Money well spent, for it rescued the recording contract from the shredder.

The song also brought the lads into contact with a benevolent Rasputin, British producer Bill Shepherd, and from first collaboration would come the sound that would later define the band. For the moment, however, the boys' problem was that they were struggling to find a uniquely Bee Gees' sound, and their second single, 'Follow the Wind', was blown to the ground almost before it got started. Whatever Barry's lyrics might intimate, there was no getting away from the fact that a teenager has not experienced the reality behind adult lyrics. That lack of authenticity was glaringly obvious when sung by kids who now barely knew of anything outside of the recording studio and the stage.

In November 1965, the Bee Gees released their first album; The Bee Gees Sing and Play 14 Barry Gibb Songs. In a sorry attempt to lend the group a songwriter who wasn't one of them, the album proved the point that the good singing and the music needed direction and focus. The 14-song album slipped humbly off into obscurity.

Another single flop made Hugh as unhappy as they boys were that they were failing to make their mark, and he accepted an offer to have them join the Spin Records label in Sydney. One of the partners, Nat Kippner, was enthusiastic about his new fledglings and gave them one of the sound studios to use for free; which was run by engineer Ossie Byrne, a Bee Gees fan. It was a Godsend and one which the Bee Gees would exploit in long sessions often stretching into the night. Maurice and Steve Kippner, Nat's son, became close friends, too, which helped.

Cushioned upon this bed of goodwill, the boys could re-assess and attack the charts anew.

In May 1966, the first recording session yielded 12 new songs, the first of 30 that year, with both Maurice and Robin putting lyrics to paper alongside Barry, and Steve assisting on vocals. Maurice was improving his bass guitar skills, and under Nat's guidance, they learned the technical joys of a good studio.

Optimism was high... but soon dashed when the first single went scuttling off red-faced after its predecessors, which made Nat delay release of the album. Again, the failure to sculpt their own niche seemed to be the stumbling block. Despite one of Barry's other songs, 'I was a Lover' being highly praised.

When the going gets tough, the tough get going, might have been the end quote to emerge from the family's deliberations at this point. Perhaps it wasn't the music that was at fault but the country. Barry in particular was unhappy at what he perceived to be the attitude towards them in their adopted land, an opinion he later revised. England was a bubbling fountain of creativity in the popular music sphere at this point, so perhaps the Bee Gees should return to the homeland and try to get into the water there.

Ironically, just as these thoughts were gaining traction in the lads' heads, they reconvened back in the studio with Nat to record one of Barry's songs that Nat felt could be the one to break the invisible barrier surrounding the boys; 'Spicks and Specks'. It was coupled with 'I Am the World', with Robin's lyrics and his trademark falsetto, a song that would earn the accolade the best record of the week from one reviewer. Nat had left behind the sparse arrangements of previous Bee Gees'; efforts and potted this single in a more lavish musical garden. The last-gasp attempt paid off. Not spectacularly, but nevertheless; though it failed to penetrate the UK and US charts, when released in September 1966, interest sent the single sailing to No. 5 in Australia.

They'd done it; finally.

They had found the golden key.

SIXTIES MEMORABILIA

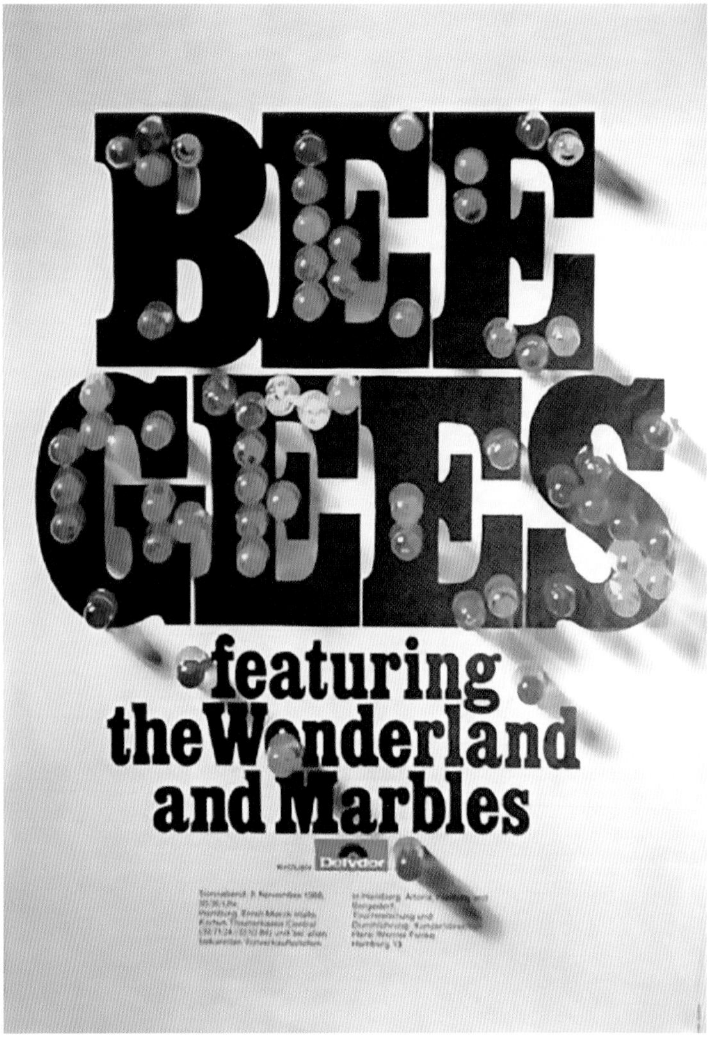

The Incredible
BEE
GEES
ARE
COMING!
with their
fabulous
'30-piece
orchestra
also featuring:
SPANKY & OUR GANG
and the NAZZ
FOREST HILLS STADIUM Sat. Aug. 10 at 8:30 PM

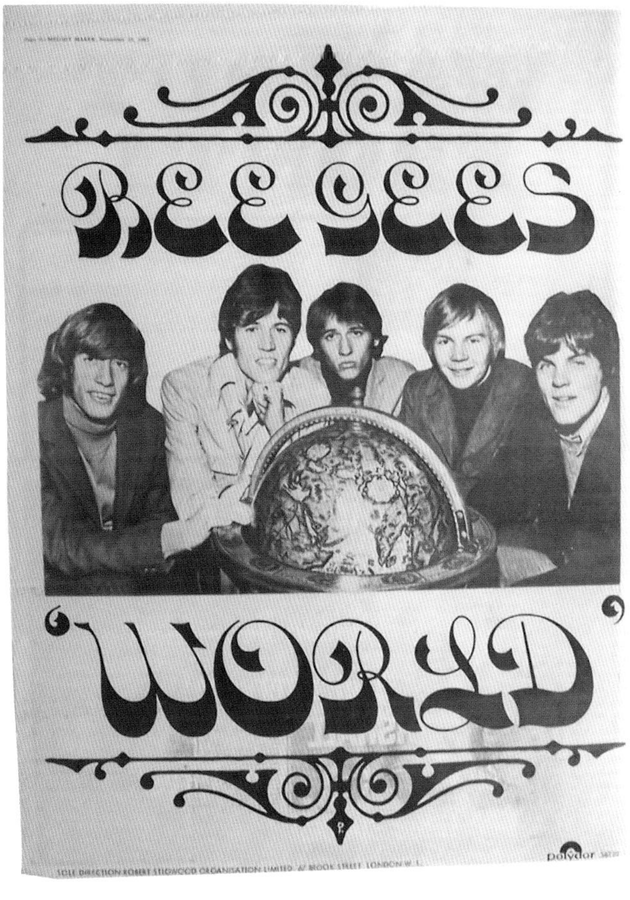
BEE GEES
'WORLD'
Polydor

PALACE
MANCHESTER
1st Performance 5-45
SUNDAY
MARCH 31
GRAND STALLS
15/-
J15
LEFT
TO BE GIVEN UP

stern präsentiert
BEE GEES in Concert '68
with the Massachusetts-String-Orchestra
guest stars:
PROCOL HARUM
Köln, Messehalle 8, 6. März 1968, 21.00 Uhr
Arrangement der Westdeutschen Konzertdirektion Köln
Block B
Reihe 3
№ 14
DM 16,–

The Robert Stigwood Organisation presents
BEE GEES
AND THEIR ORCHESTRA
Conductor:
BILL SHEPHERD
GRAPEFRUIT
SPECIAL GUEST STARS
DAVE DEE, DOZY, BEAKY, MICK & TICH
ABC CHESTER
ON THE STAGE
Saturday, 30th March at 6.15 & 8.30
ONE NIGHT ONLY
All Seats bookable in advance
Stalls: 15/- 12/6 10/- 7/6
Circle: 12/6 10/- 7/6

KONZERTHAUS STUTTGARTER LIEDERHALLE
BEETHOVENSAAL
hans werner funke, hamburg
Stadt Stuttgart
stern präsentiert
Freitag, 1. März 1968, 21 Uhr
Bee Gees in Concert '68
Einschl. MwSt.
DM 13.—
Parkett
RECHTS MITTE
Reihe 20
Platz 65

BERLINER SPORTPALAST
1 Berlin 30 Potsdamer Straße 170/172
Parkett
Donnerstag, 7. März 1968, 20 Uhr
DM
14,00
stern präsentiert
BEE GEES IN CONCERT '68
Arrangement: Sportpalast GmbH
Programmänderungen vorbehalten
Kartenrücknahme ausgeschlossen
Oberfinanzdirektion Berlin
1. Mittel-
Parkett
rechts
Reihe 6
Platz 01
DM 14,—
incl. 10% Mehrwertsteuer
7. 3. 68

16th August, 1969
1/-
Fabulous 208
ROBIN
GIBB
NOW!
FREE CASUALS COMPETITION! WIN 2 SOLID GOLD WATCHES!
SIX FAB FOOTBALLERS
RADIO LUXEMBOURG PROGRAMMES 12th–18th AUGUST

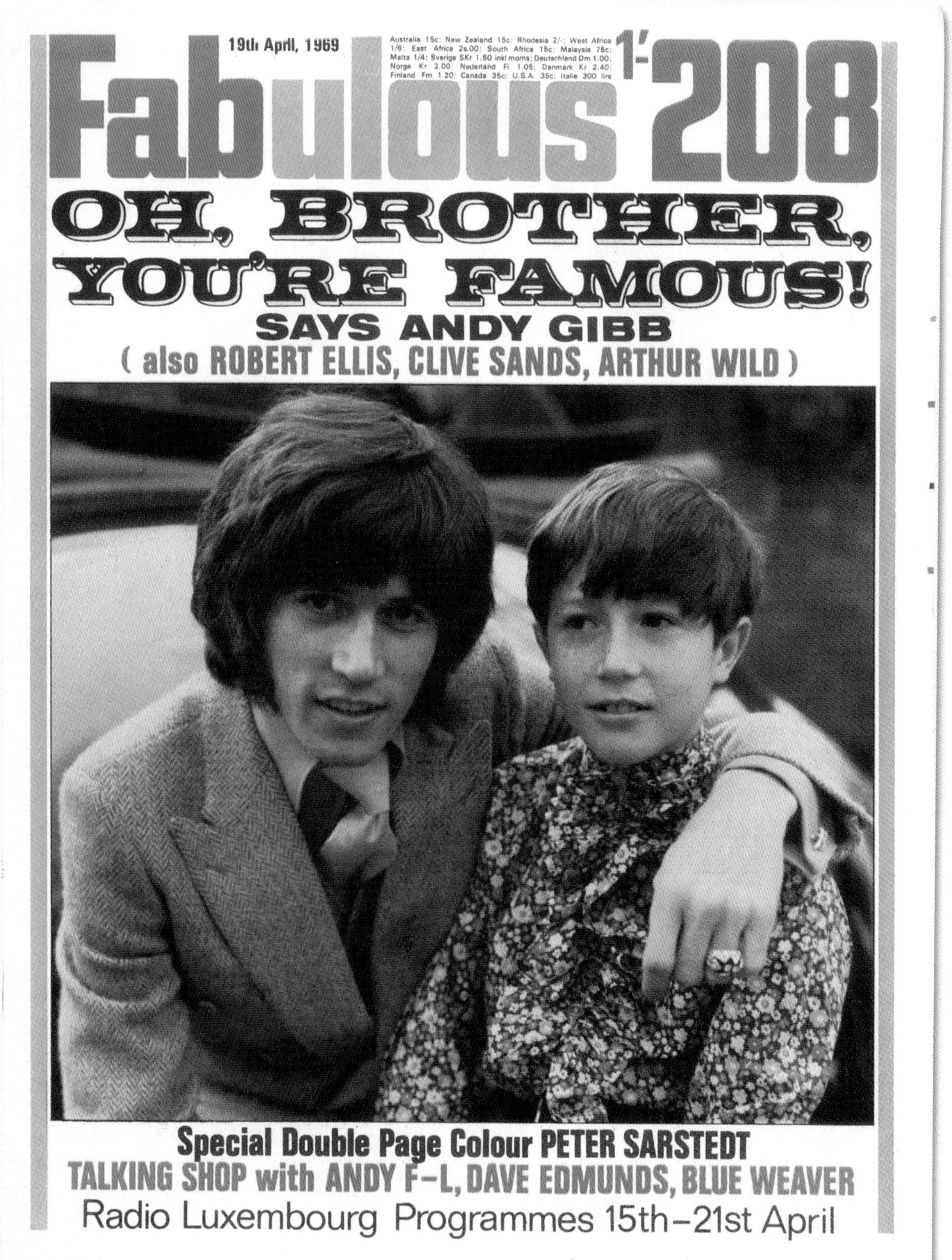

19th April, 1969

Australia 15c; New Zealand 15c; Rhodesia 2/-; West Africa 1/6; East Africa 2s.00; South Africa 15c; Malaysia 75c; Malta 1/4; Sverige SKr 1.60 inkl moms; Deutschland Dm 1.00; Norge Kr 2.00; Nederland Fl 1.05; Danmark Kr 2.40; Finland Fm 1.20; Canada 35c; U.S.A. 35c; Italie 300 lire

Fabulous 1/- 208

OH, BROTHER, YOU'RE FAMOUS!

SAYS ANDY GIBB

(also ROBERT ELLIS, CLIVE SANDS, ARTHUR WILD)

Special Double Page Colour PETER SARSTEDT

TALKING SHOP with ANDY F–L, DAVE EDMUNDS, BLUE WEAVER

Radio Luxembourg Programmes 15th–21st April

14th December, 1968
1/-
Fabulous 208
GET TAKEN FOR A RIDE
WITH MAURICE & SOME
OTHER DISHY PEOPLE
SPECIAL PAINTING FOR
YOUR BEDROOM WALL!
4 PAGES OF FANTASTIC
CHRISTMAS GIFTS
IN COLOUR:
JAMES DRURY
GOES LION
HUNTING
RADIO LUXEMBOURG
PROGS 10th–16th DEC.
ROLLS ROYCE

29th March, 1969
Australia 15c; New Zealand 15c; Rhodesia 2/-; West Africa 1/6; East Africa 2s.00; South Africa 15c; Malaysia 75c; Malta 1/4; Sverige SKr 1.50 inkl moms; Deutschland Dm 1.00; Norge Kr 2.00; Naderland Fl 1.05; Danmark Kr 2.40; Finland Fm 1.20; Canada 35c; U.S.A. 35c; Italie 300 lire
1'-
Fabulous '208
"HANG ON TO YOUR SKIRTS"
SAYS DAVE DEE
"GOD? WHO KNOWS?"
ASKS KENNY EVERETT
MOVE-IN CLOSE UP
RADIO LUXEMBOURG PROGRAMMES 25th–31st. MARCH
MAURICE & LULU
IN SUPER DOUBLE PAGE COLOUR

BACK FROM THE CLIFF EDGE

Barry was married. He tied the knot on the 22nd of August 1966 at the age of 19 with the secretary of the boys' fan club, Maureen Bates. They lived together but a short time and would divorce in 1970. He was also now writing solely for a publishing company run by father Hugh and his partner Norman Whitely, and in November that year, Hugh did something that would fan the Bee Gees' spark into a searing flame and cause an earthquake in the lives of all concerned with Bee Gees music; he took three of the 40 songs that Barry had pumped out in the preceding months and sent the acetate off to Brian Epstein at NEMS in Britain, which is where the lads were now resolved to head after the success of their single. From then on, they could never decide which country was truly home.

In January of the new year of 1967, the Gibbs sailed off on a 5-week trip that they hoped would lead to a fresh new life gilded with success. For bed and board and sustained by Benzedrine (a forerunner of alcohol, Maurice's future bedfellow), they sang their way over the oceans; 'Yellow Submarine' was the favourite; the wires were already connecting up, as they were to find out.

NEMS was the company that managed the Epstein businesses in the UK, and Brian Epstein had engaged another Aussie, Robert Stigwood, to run it. It was Stigwood's hands that first grasped those acetate recordings sent from Hugh, and he then had Paul McCartney listen to them. "Sign them, they're great" was Paul's response. Without them knowing, the Bee Gees' old lives had just vanished behind them.

As luck would have it, the Bee Gees were finally in the right place at the right time. Not that it seemed that way at the time. Almost broke and based in Hendon, North London, the Gibbs re-entered an England that was glowing with the light of Carnaby St., Pink Floyd, and the Beatles. And, fortunately for the brothers, there was also that Mr. Stigwood. And he wanted to see them. For an audition, which ended with Stigwood telling them to get themselves to his office.

"Can we do business?" were the encouraging words they heard in the NEMS building. Stigwood as manager, publisher and record label for a 5-year term. The Gibbs would be straitjacketed; but in the musical home of the Beatles, that was some straitjacket. And Stigwood believed in them and would push his protégés to outdo even the Beatles. And it was also a straitjacket that Stigwood wanted the boys to decorate with some Carnaby St. colour. Which they duly did.

From March through into April of 1967, Stigwood hired session musicians and got the lads to work on recording demos of the Bee Gees' own work. From those sessions emerged the single that would provide them with their first entry into the top 20. 'The New York Mining Disaster' title was not exactly a conventional hit title, and the song was buoyed by a restrained musical arrangement. The boys looked like wannabe Beatles (and indeed, everybody thought they were they Beatles when the single was released, a confusion which did them no harm) in their Carnaby St. credentials; but Barry was on an emotional high in 'To Love Somebody', and the single made its way to No 12 in the UK and 14 in the US. A good start by anyone's standards.

A sign that the Bee Gees were in amongst the big boys and girls was an appearance on Britain's Top of The Pops TV show with one of Britain's top poppers, Lulu. Ever sharp, Stigwood took the opportunity to suggest to the world that Maurice and she were on 'good terms'. Which they soon were, becoming king and queen of the world according to Lulu. Robin, too, was in the dating game having hitched up with Stigwood's secretary, Molly.

Stigwood had also negotiated a recording deal in the US with Atlantic Records' ATCO worth in excess of $200,000,

RIGHT:
Bee Gees portrait, 1967

RIGHT:
Robert Stigwood, extreme left, with some fellow directors of his new firm including the Bee Gees, Frankie Howerd, Beryl Virtue and writers Ray Galton and Alan Simpson. February 1968

and was letting the world know that the next big things had arrived in Britain. But he had not reckoned with his inexperienced charges, who, flushed with sudden success, blurted out in an interview that they had never wanted to go to Australia in the first place and hated being compared to the Beatles. Clang. Much hasty repair work was needed before that slight was forgiven.

And it quickly was. For when the first British album was swiftly released in July of 1967, entitled Bee Gees 1st, it swam to No. 10 down under. It also broke the top ten in both the UK and the US at 8 and 7 respectively.
The sound was not the Bee Gees of old; swathed in

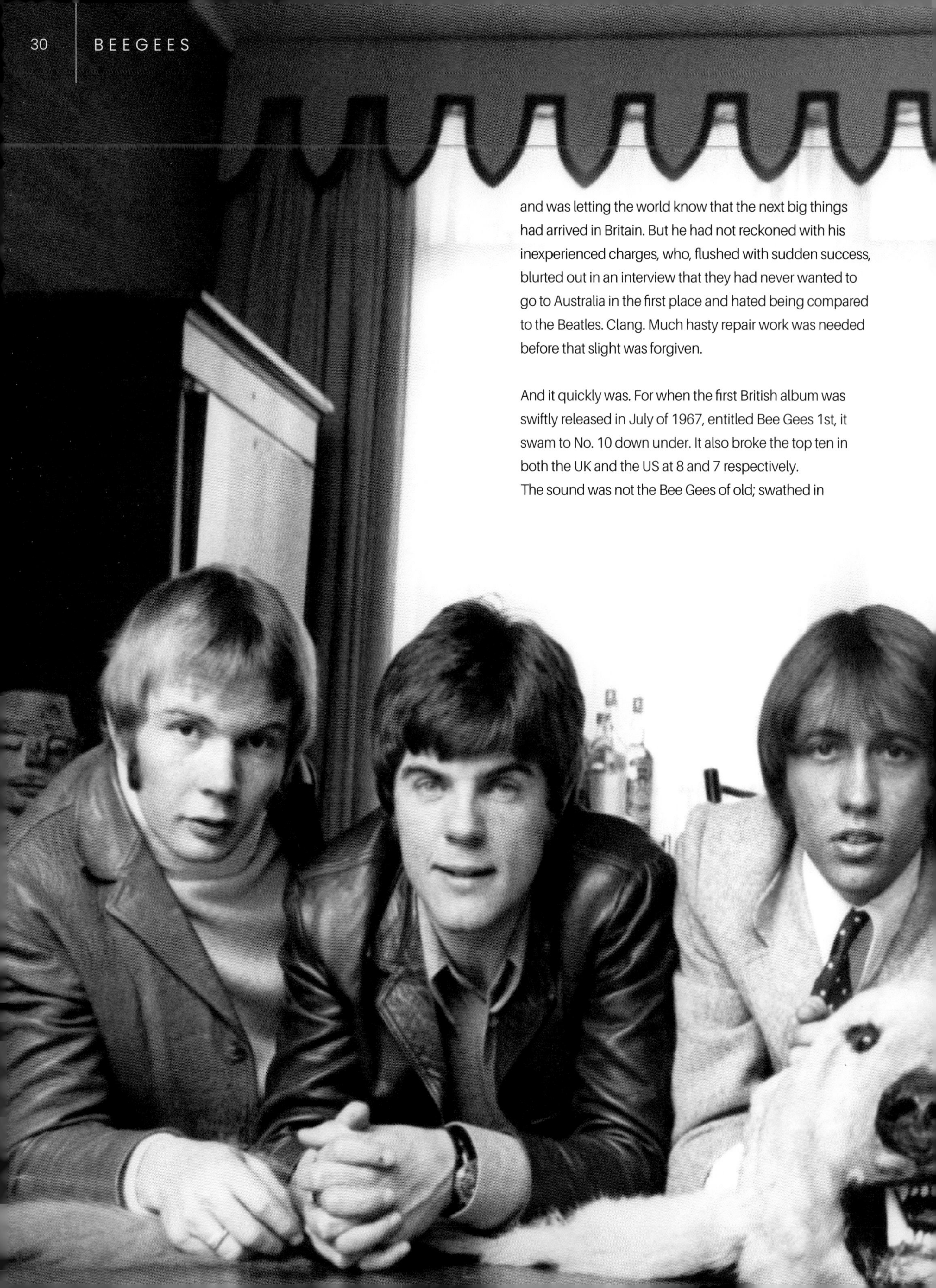

orchestrations and psychedelic pop, it attracted the epithet 'baroque', and even the album cover designed by Klaus Voorman of Beatles' fame indicated a group meshed into the sound machine at the centre of British pop culture and now assaulting the heights.

This heady take off suddenly received a cold blast when the news came in the Brian Epstein had overdosed and at 32 years of age, was dead.

Stigwood, whose behaviour had been causing friction in NEMS before Brian's death, now learned that his term at NEMS was over. He departed, much richer, and took the Bee Gees with him; fortunately for them, ready to forge them into megastars.

With the release of their single 'Massachusetts', recorded over just two days, Stigwood must have been extremely happy, for with Robin's lead vocals showing what he was truly capable of and Bill Shepherd working his orchestral magic, the song unexpectedly brought a No. 1 spot in the UK and several other countries, and the money started rolling in.

Stigwood then had them shipped off to the States. Barry remembers the boys writing the song about a place they

MAIN IMAGE:
L-R: Colin Petersen, Vince Melouney, Maurice Gibb, Barry Gibb, Robin Gibb, 1966

MAIN IMAGE:
L-R Vince Melouney, Barry Gibb, Maurice Gibb, Colin Petersen and Robin Gibb, 1966

had never been to, because Massachusetts sounded good; they had tuned into the sense of an idealised home that was so strong in the States, where travelling hippies bathed in songs of yearning for places far away. Stigwood must also have been rejoicing that they didn't sell the song to the Australian group The Seekers as they had intended to.

The Bee Gees had cracked the jackpot and were walking on air, and they used their fame as most pop groups did, to fund wine, women and merriment, much to the displeasure of Barry's wife, of course. But his marriage was going nowhere. It was around this time that Barry fell under the spell of former Miss Edinburgh, Linda Gray, the woman who would take him away from Maureen and with whom he would spend the rest of his life fathering five children.

Maurice, not yet out of his teens, took to the bottle like a pro. The boys were the toast of the town and were introduced to the British musical elite, groups such as the Who, the Beatles or the Stones. And London's Saville Theatre hosted them replete with a 30-piece orchestra.

They reinforced their claim to this elite club by producing another two top ten hit singles before the year was out; 'Worlds' and 'Words'. They reached 9 and 8 in the UK respectively with 'Worlds' coming in at 15 in the US. 'Worlds' and 'Words' scored No. 1 spots in Germany, and hugged the first and second spots in several other European countries, too.

'Jumbo', their final single release of the year, got stuck in the mid-20s in both the UK and the US, whilst striking the

fifth spot in Germany.

A year of superlatives, a truly comet-like ascendency into stardom that had Stigwood blowing the boys' trumpet and proclaiming that the Bee Gees would be as big as the Beatles; just different.

So they entered the year of 1968 exhausted, but in high spirits and expectancy. There was no respite from the merry-go-round once you were on it, and there was a new album to record amidst consideration of a film and a TV special. Life was parties, work, recording, money for luxuries, expensive cars especially. And even before the new album was finished, the Bee Gees were eyeing the

spoils to be had in America, so an appearance on American TV's Smothers Brothers Comedy Hour was booked to raise their profile there. But as they swung into stardom, the destructive Gollum lurking beneath the glamorous surface was on the move.

The new album was ready for release in February. Titled Horizon, it contained a side-swiping imitation of the Beatles' 'Strawberry Fields' called, 'Lemons Never Forget' ("The lemon sings my song. He's known it all along"), an attack on the "Junior Rivals" tag that had been attached to the brothers. The album made its way to No.16 in the UK and 12 in the US with reviews and fan reception both mixed. Germany, ever faithful, saw them rise to the No. 1 spot.

"A poignant, even somber yet gorgeous ballad filled with clever lyrics" was one comment on the track 'World'. Amongst others' descriptions of "cheerful" and "pretty" songs, though, Rolling Stone were damning with faint praise; "Sixties jukebox love songs". Somewhat wide of the mark as far as the track 'Really and Sincerely' was concerned, for it was born from Robin walking away from a train crash in South London in the UK in which 49 of his fellow passengers were killed.

The Bee Gees seemed to be flooding over the music market. TV, radio, concerts rolled into one another; master American TV chat show host Ed Sullivan presented them on his show prior to the boys undertaking the first full-scale UK tour with a launch at the Albert Hall in London in March. Their Ed Sullivan appearance, a starchy performance and not a particularly happy experience, presaged what was about to happen next.

The Bee Gees were now preparing to blitz the States in July with a tour that Stigwood told the world would earn them $1,000,000. Well, not quite.

Barely had they started before they cancelled dates at the end of July. Exhaustion was the reason put forward, although their appearance at a recording studio to work on new songs rather quashed that protestation. Empty seats at venues was the real reason, and as the cancelled dates

MAIN IMAGE:
The Bee Gees perform on Top Of The Pops, 1968

MAIN IMAGE:
Rehearsing for a television program broadcasted for the end of year holidays and produced by Belgian television, around October 1968

piled up into a car crash, Stigwood pulled the plug on the tour. Years would pass before a second attempt was made at a conquering heroes act.

Still, at least a wave of success washed in their direction with the release of their single 'I've Gotta Get a Message to You' (Robin's saunter into the mind of a man on Death Row), which climbed to No. 1 in the UK and 8 in the States when released in September 1968, belying, once more, the claim that they only penned drip-pop.

September was also the month that another album, Idea, hit the stores. It fared well in the UK at No. 4, though only just entering the US top 20 at No. 17.

Lead guitarist Vince Melouney wrote and sang on 'Such a Shame, the only song not written by one of the brothers on any of their studio albums. Vince would soon depart the band in frustration at the forced retardation of his song writing skills, an indication of problems elsewhere within the band. For the success of the album disguised a serious crack that had appeared within the group. After a decade of incessant closeness, alcohol, the amount of individual creative input, or Barry's assumed head-of-the-clan role,

had all served to taint the gloss. Barry recalled that "We were in friction at that point. We weren't getting on... not getting along very well, and egos. Ego, I think, is the key word for this group".

Stigwood wasn't about to let up digging in his gold mine, even though the album Idea encapsulated the group's splintering; only four songs were collaborations. Stigwood wanted still more; he wanted enormous; he wanted a rock opera. He ended up with a recalcitrant parrot that almost blew the band out of the jungle and caused a temporary rift with Robin.

The great project was designed to be a concept album, a rock opera along the lines of The Who's Tommy, one that would suit a spectacular stage production and therefore please Stigwood, though it ended up as a collection of disparate songs and styles ranging from lush orchestration to psychedelic and country. The theme would centre around a man on an iceberg after a shipwreck, whose wife has absconded with a vicar who is also the narrator.

Recording began with 'I Laugh in Your Face' on the 12th of July 1968 and the project was eventually christened Odessa.

MAIN IMAGE:

Rehearsing for a television program broadcasted for the end of year holidays and produced by Belgian television, around October 1968

It proved a hard task for a band that was at loggerheads to produce a cohesive product. Arguments bubbled, concentration was lost and verbal knives were thrown. The brothers rarely met in the studio, and Barry was often the lone GIbb completing mixes and wondering what it was all for. Stigwood was concentrating more time on his musical Hair, and then left for America, which didn't help matters.

Vince Melouney gathered his guitar and left in November 1968 after eight sessions realising his time was up. "I have never really felt 100 percent a Bee Gee. The talent I have doesn't come up to the standard of the Gibb brothers talent... my ideas don't augment their ideas."

Colin Petersen would not be far behind.

In the middle of all this there were concerts, and on the 4th of December came Robin's marriage to Molly Hullis. Not to be outdone, Maurice announced a few days later that he and Lulu were to wed, too.

Not yet 19, Robin was so upset that his choice for the single release, 'Lamplight', had been ignored (the single chosen, 'The First of May', although a fast riser was equally fast at vanishing) that sibling rivalry overwhelmed him and he left the group after the album release leaving a hiatus for a whole year. Convinced that Stigwood was favouring Barry and grooming him for leadership of the group, Robin even got a new phone number and let loose the threat of taking his songs from the album. Neither was he backward in letting the press know of his displeasure. With a united front against him, he was informed brusquely that he had a contract with three years unexpired and couldn't leave. This was a double whammy for the Gibbs; the break up of a dream they had hungered for and the fracturing of close family ties. For many years after the incident, Robin still found the memories difficult to deal with.

As the enmity rose to its climax, Maurice and 20-year-old Lulu got married at Gerrard's Cross in Buckinghamshire, England. Despite Barry's objections on the grounds that they were too young. It was February 1969, and Lulu wore

her trademark mini, in silk. Their best man was Robin. Barry, with his own relationship problems with Linda Gray looming in his mind and informing his opinions on marriage, was to prove correct in his assessment of the married couple. They were to have but a few years together.

Over 1,000 fans crowded the small church and police had to keep the crowds at bay as a white-suited Maurice impatiently waited for his bride's green Rolls to turn up. She could barely get through the throng when she did, but made her way through the police cordon to vanish inside the church where Barry, having relented, had joined his siblings. 30 minutes later, Mr. and Mrs. Gibb emerged to struggle through the crowds again.

The double album would probably have enjoyed life more had it been reduced to one, for there are several weak links in the song chain; 'You'll Never See My Face Again' or 'I Laugh in Your Face' sitting uneasily with 'Lamplight' or 'Black Diamond'. The lyric writing, too, left reviewers with the sense of a band trying too hard to give emergency resuscitation to the baby after a difficult birth. It was an album that captured the quirky, sometimes incomprehensible, panorama of writing that was the Bee Gees, and the title song – at over 7 minutes long, the longest of any Bee Gees composition to date – included flamenco, cello, and wordless Gregorian chant like-vocals; and Stigwood loved it.

To compound the agony, upon release in March 1969, the album was a critical flop; "over-inflated, pseudo-cinematic arrangements"; though many thought it a masterpiece, too, their Sgt. Pepper moment, and it reached up to hit No. 10 in the UK, 4 in Germany and 20 in the States. It has since come to be regarded as a classic album.

But Odessa represented a deep cleft in the Bee Gees' careers. Only in 1975 would they again see the inside of the top twenty. The brothers' close bonds had been severed, and even with Stigwood, the honeymoon was over.

Barry insisted that the Bee Gees lived on.

It would have been more accurate to say that the Bee Gees were hobbling on. The remaining brothers recorded without him and appeared in public singing with their sister in Robin's place. There was a brief reappearance of the lost twin on Top of the Pops; but then it was over. Robin kept the press informed of what he was and wasn't going to do, whilst Stigwood issued a writ against him – to shut him up, more than intending anything more serious.

With the release of the Odessa album in March came Robin's announcement that put paid to any hopes of reconciliation; he was going solo under his own management, Bow and Arrow. "Music to me is an adventure, and I can do far more on my own. It was restricting writing for the Bee Gees, but I enjoyed it until they began to judge what I was doing."

Although nervous exhaustion and a minor breakdown were floated to the world to excuse Robin's absence from the band's public appearances, the rift was intensifying. Barry was in no mood to climb down from his indignant perch, either, and whilst leaving the door open for a return, insisted Robin would have to come to him first. Maurice found himself jammed in the centre of this war of the egos and bore no ill will towards Robin. In fact, he would soon go to the studio to join in with Robin's first solo single and add harmonies and instrumentals. Maurice was sensitive to the situation and had known that Robin had never seen eye-to-eye with Colin and Vince and had often criticised them even on stage.

There was another problem that Robin's walk-out had caused; the Talk of The Town appearance in London. Stigwood came to the rescue again with another idea.

There was another Gibb; sister Lesley.

"Out of the blue, I got a call from Rob and he said ;Lesley, can you sing?'" Lesley recalled in later years. "I made light

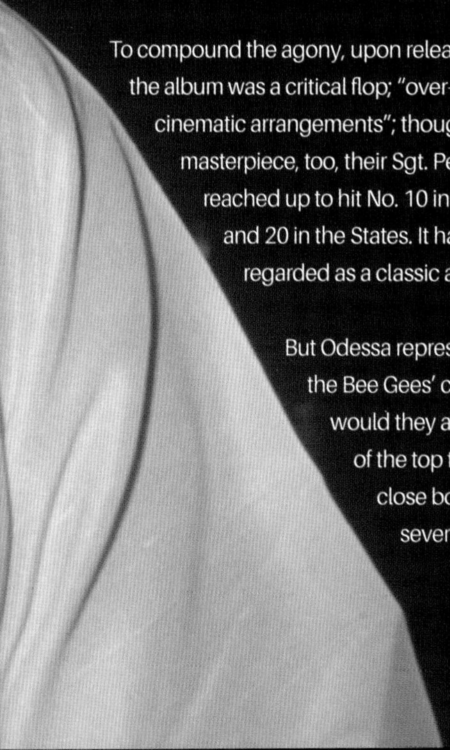

MAIN IMAGE:
Barry Gibb, April 1969

MAIN IMAGE:
Bee Gees perform on Top of the Pops, 6th March 1969

of it and said, 'Well, can't everyone sing?'".

Inexperienced and with three weeks of rehearsals in front of her, 24-year-old Lesley, who only a month earlier had given birth to twins, found herself singing alongside her famous brothers.

On the 27th of April, the show was ready for recording.

Wearing a little gold dress on the day, Leslie remembered that she "was petrified, all those people watching, I almost burst into tears". But she wasn't too stunned to enjoy it. "It was amazing. I loved it on the night... our harmonies as Gibb family members sounded very much the same... I know Robin watched it and he said he felt very choked up about it... but it wasn't for me. I had my twins to get back to...".

Lesley asked Robin why he didn't return to the group, and once it was all over she returned to the quieter life in Australia that she preferred, with her husband and twins. Robin was still gripped by the perceived injury to his 19-year-old ego.

His new single was 'Saved by the Bell', a song of loss in which Robin's voice soared upwards and softened hearts as he confessed that "I cried for you".

Poignant was hardly the word. Not a new direction, but a new beginning.

The UK charts were treated to Robin's single and the rump Bee Gees' latest, 'Don't Forget to Remember' in the charts simultaneously. The Bee Gees offering managed to hit No. 2 in the UK and No. 1 in three other territories, whilst Robin took the No. 2 spot in the UK and also the No. 1 spot in three other territories. So Robin must have felt vindicated, his point had been proven.

Irked, possibly, Barry took to spreading the news that the Bee Gees were on the lookout for a Robin replacement. Jack Bruce, ex-Cream singer, was mentioned. Hardly a serious contender with that background. Barry seemed to be fanning the flames of his ire in public hoping to hit Robin's ears, only to confess later that it was nigh on impossible to replace the lost brother. The private feud of the brothers Gibb was scattered confetti-like into the public conscience. Stigwood had to clear up the messy details, but kept the ties to Robin strong by assigning him PR manager Chris Hutchins, and also Vic Lewis, one of the managers from his own organisation, the Robert Stigwood Organisation, besides arranging for Robin's publishing company to be administered by RSO, too.

Robin had always been considered the spiky brother, a complicated character; sudden success had not smoothed him out. His ego did not allow him to be second fiddle to anyone, and slights, imagined or real, produced weeds that were a long time withering. In his own head, he was the equal of Bob Dylan and wasn't about to wait around pining. He could be far more productive on his own he knew. He was full of ideas and energy, bursting to get his solo career on the road; he was going to work on a book, a Christmas special, two screenplays and musical scores, one a reworking of Dickens' A Christmas Carol, another about Henry VIII. He was already planning his first solo album, Robin's Reign, which he would record starting in March 1969 and finalise in October of that year, and he wrote another two songs. 'Moon Anthem' and 'Ghost of Christmas Past', which were never released. The album would contain tracks that were pure Bee Gees; 'August Gone', for example, one of the singles from the album, but it was noted in reviews that the lyrical content as a whole, despite being rooted in the Bee Gees' comfort zone of love, reflected a deep sadness.

Robin and his brothers, indeed, his whole family, remained out of touch that year, though Robin would readily send out stingers to the press if their pens came anywhere near him, and the animosity ran deep, with vague threats constantly lurking in the background to toxify the atmosphere.

Meanwhile, the brothers too had attempted to recruit a

new singer, Peter Mason, but the attempt never had the Stigwood seal of approval and fizzled out; Stigwood was quietly working to get the trio back together again, but wisely allowing them the space they needed to get the claustrophobia out of their ego systems and let family blood ties kick in again.

Undaunted by events – "Since Robin left, Barry and I are a lot closer" said Maurice, "we're working much more together" – the Bee Gees remainers started to work on recording their own album in May 1969. This was Cucumber Castle, the only Bee Gees album without Robin – the Australians stayed loyal and gave it a No. 10 perch, but the Americans barely allowed it into the top 100, and the Brits didn't allow it into their top 50. Friction had not gone away and Colin Petersen, who thought that the band without Robin was doomed to failure, was duly ejected from the group in September. Now there were only two of the original Bee Gees' lineup left standing. It was another messy, unpleasant incident, which led to a writ and court case, and a rueful Barry revealing much later that it was Stigwood who had been responsible for firing Colin, adding that their sound had suffered because of it.

Cucumber Castle recording was all but over by that eventful September with Terry Cox from Pentangle finishing the drum parts. There was a TV special named after the album, a kitsch-laden, feathery, armour-weighted, Tudor-age roustabout that managed to coerce Richard Harris – "Get me out of here" – Eric Clapton, comedian Frankie Howerd, Spike Milligan and Lulu into a gooey filmic soup. Robin must have been overjoyed that he had opted out.

The Cucumber Castle album had just two tracks to recommend it; 'Don't Forget to Remember' and 'Bury Me Down by the River', though that song still longed for Robin's brilliant vocals to add the razor blade-emotional strike.

So the protracted guerrilla warfare continued as the separated limbs of the Bee Gees' body wriggled on through to the last month of the 60s decade, all three of the boys furiously working through studio time as though they might never sell another record. Robin kept the speed he consumed balanced with downers, Maurice kept the drink flowing and Barry smoked his cares away.

Barry and Maurice tried to keep the body going on life support with 'I.O.I.O.' and 'If I Only Had My Mind on Something Else', from Cucumber Castle, but they both ran out of breath and crashed to earth shortly after scrambling into the US 100 and the UK top 50. Symbolically, Barry and Maurice's US tour failed to materialise. Finally, deprived of air, the body expired. Barry could take no more and decided that he, too, was going to be an ex-Bee Gee. It was December 1969, and the group formerly announced that they had split. They would all go solo. The dream had faded.

Barry wrote songs throughout January to be ready to record his first solo album in February and March 1970. The album acquired an unofficial name; The Kid's No Good, but never saw the light of day. At least Barry's mind was creatively occupied in what must have been a dredging period of his life. His marriage, too, was lying in the dust. In July of that year, Barry and his first wife, Maureen Bates, finally divorced. It had been a brief sojourn; they had known one another for just under four years at the time of the decree absolute. The way was clear to seal a longer-lasting union later that year with Linda Gray.

MAIN IMAGE:
Robin Gibb, April 1969

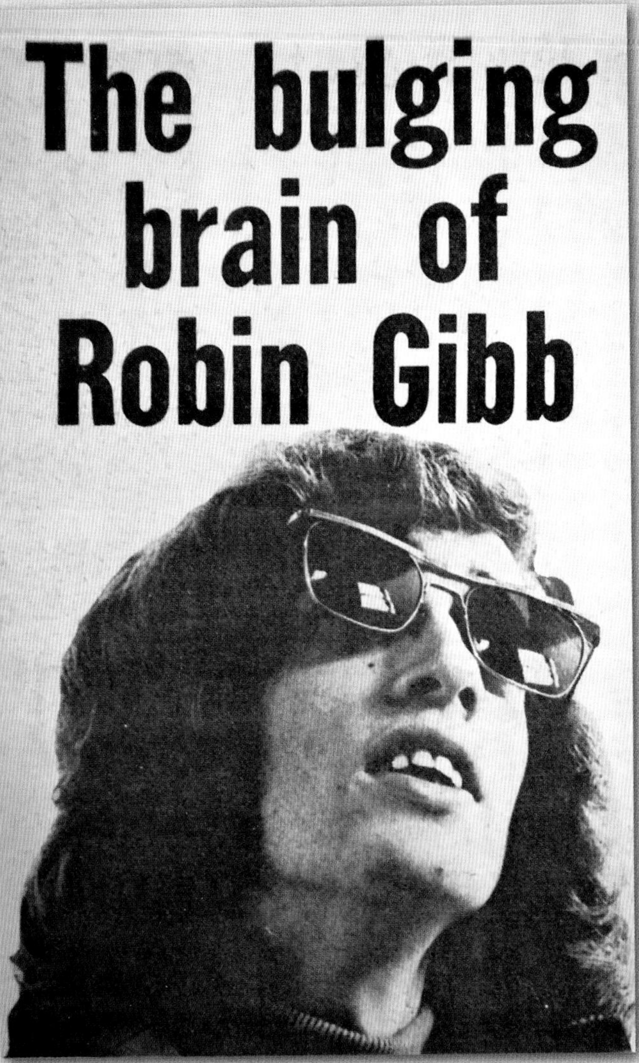

to the commercial viability of the songwriting. The others were destined for the bootleggers.

What more poignant symbolism of this era of a dream escaping than Robin and Maurice also producing still-born albums; Robin's was Sing Slowly Sisters (finally released in 2015), whilst Maurice worked on The Loner.

There were one-off performances; on the 31st of January and the 1st of February 1970, Robin was on stage in Auckland, New Zealand. Barry went to Germany for the Miss Teen Princess of the World pageant in June. The Brothers Grim trying to present the Brothers Cheery and throwing out contradictory statements about the state of play in the family and what they were about to do next, as though scared that if they didn't tell the world that all was right and dandy, reality would drag them into the Slough of Despond.

In April, Maurice released his first solo single, 'Railroad', which, tellingly, was big in Malaysia, where it came in at No. 6, not appearing in the charts in the US or Australia. It was a piano-heavy, rather plodding pseudo-country number that lacked the soaring vocals that would lay on the sentimentality heavily enough to make everyone cry. He would only release his second single in 1984 with a Jim Reeves-like 'Hold Her in Your Hand".

Robin was also writing for Welsh singer Tom Jones, and finding that being a solo artist wasn't the summit of all things after all; the fun had leeched away. His album – sumptuous pop arrangements by Kenny Clayton based on Robin's melodies played on an organ, guitar and drums – although not a chart success, proved that the talent was undimmed and the voice had the power to affect the listener as powerfully as ever; also that Gibb Brothers writing could aspire to the heights of the Beatles – if channelled correctly. The hiatus had proven loud and clear that the Bee Gees produced hit songs; but only together. As solo artists, they had become uninspired and the voices lacked impact. The only problem was how to paste the torn egos back together again. Stigwood was indulging his stars in the hope that these young men, even Barry was only 24 at the time, would somehow understand where

Otherwise he would spend his time in his flat brooding, whilst Maurice hit the night spots and caroused with celebrity mates, Ringo Starr especially, if he wasn't helping him in the studio, and Robin tried to make his solo career grow legs.

The tracks on Barry's album owed much to the singer's love for country and western of the Australian variety and were later described as 'moody' and 'Beatle-esque', with Bill Shepherd working his magic with the arrangements. The tear-jerker 'I'll Kiss Your Memory' released as a single in May with 'This Time' on the B-side, failed to ignite at all. Ballads and soul influence mingled with typical Bee Gees output, and although the songs were never released by Barry, the many 'covers' that went into circulation testified

RIGHT:
Bee Gees portrait, 1970

the reality of their predicament lay and wrestle their egos to the ground for the good of all concerned. But for how long would he support them with the evidence of their failures piling up mercilessly?

The answer to his prayers came in mid-year 1970. Rumours leaked from the Stigwood Organisation that the boys would be coming back together sooner rather than later. Those egos, it seemed, had suffered a severe talking to, with help from the record-buying public, no doubt. Robin and Maurice had already been recording songs together again having entered the studio on the 7th of June and again on the 21st. Barry was hesitant at first when he remembered that he picked up the phone one day when holidaying in Spain and heard his brother Robin's voice; "Let's do it again."

Robin wanted sole credit for songs he alone had written; one of the original stumbling blocks. And he rather wanted to see if his solo creations would prove that he was more bankable than brothers 2 and 3.

But Barry, too, was fed up working with non-family members and was longing for a hit. He may have needed a little persuasion to forget the ugliness of the past months, but he did, and the brothers got together to discuss what had happened and what could happen now, so that by the 21st of August, the sweetness and light had returned. On the 24th August, the world was told that the Bee Gees were back. There was even a public apology given to Robin by Maurice in Melody Maker for all that had been said about him, as an indication of the sincerity of the reunion. Barry was awash with enthusiasm as great as his resentment had been previously; "We weren't cut out to be solo stars, we were cut out to be the Bee Gees. Somebody in his almighty wisdom knew that, whether we did or not." And with a flourish he declared, "The Bee Gees are there and they will never, ever part again. We are a musical establishment." Rather forgetting his strong desire to prove himself as a solo artist.

They lost no time in getting back into the studio with renewed relish to work on an album and the elusive hit song that would announce their renaissance. With former The Groove drummer Geoff Bridgford on board, they took themselves off to Morgan Studios in London for recording sessions that would become the album 2 Years On. Whilst it fared only moderately in the US and UK at 33 and 32 respectively, the uncoupled single 'Lonely Days' – with some help from promotional appearances on Johnny Carsen's Tonight Show, The Johnny Cash Show, The Dick Cavett Show, The Ed Sullivan Show and The Andy Williams Show during the Bee Gees' tour – hit No. 3 in the US and No. 1 in Canada, although it lounged at 33 in the UK. What was good enough for the Beatles was inspiration for the Bee Gees, and 'Lonely Days', with its creative twists, abrupt tempo changes and melancholic harmonies, could easily have slipped out of Abbey Road Studios. Nonetheless, proof, if any were needed, that the sum of the Brothers Gibb was better than the individual parts, and they still had the talent, sparkle and vocal ability to hit the heights.

Barry sealed his happiness that year when, on the 1st of September 1970, he married Linda Gray. They would have five children together, Stephen Ashley, Travis, Michael and Alexandra.

The album 2 Years On was released in November 1970 with only three songs that were collaborations by the three brothers; 'Lonely Days', 'Man For All Seasons' and 'Back Home'. The others had been worked on by Robin and Maurice before the great reunion took place, and Barry wrote four of his own. It was far from being a new Abbey Road, and its low sales confirmed that, although it was rich in harmonic inventiveness and solid pop arrangements. They had signalled their intentions with what AllMusic later called a "surprisingly hard-edged" album that was "somewhat less fey and more progressive", praising the general quality of the production and the move away from the gloomier iterations of themselves that had pervaded past albums.

There was a genetic problem, though, that came to light after the initial burst of energy, and the astute Stigwood noticed it when the brothers began to work on their next round of songs. One reviewer had also pointed a finger at it, rather unwelcomely, when writing about 2 Years On. The Bee Gee formula was growing stale; yet the brothers

LEFT:
First united venture in nearly two years, 1970

blithely ignored the warning signs or thought that they were false alarms.

In the new year of 1971, they set out for their first proper America tour and concluded with a two-week run in New York at the Philharmonic Hall. Which, despite being described as "impeccably perfect", turned out be rather less than a success. Fortunately, the boys did not allow their single 'How Can You Mend a Broken Heart' to be released by Andy Williams, because their own version took the number one spot in July, rather maintaining the illusion, if somewhat tenuously, that all was well in the land of harmony.

The Beatles were now mirages inhabiting the past, for the singer-songwriter's day had arrived. That was where the Gibbs excelled; they could write fast and anywhere, but seemed never to be credited as part of that genre. Even when they hit No 1. Perhaps their "abstract and indirect lyrics" as one writer described them, were to blame. Certainly their straddling of musical styles was on the list of indictments, their 'failure' to remain within one specific genre, aiming, instead, for a widely inclusive listener base.

The repaired Bee Gees resumed the former status quo of Bee Gees mark I; Robin and Barry assumed lead vocals with the exception of Maurice's solo songs. But something seemed to have changed subtly, the rupture had altered them. Robin, in particular, it was noted, seemed to have lost a certain sharpness. He abandoned instruments, singing with just a microphone. Barry played his guitar, with Maurice crafting the Bee Gees' music sphere on piano, bass and guitar and having a hand in the arrangements, as well. This was where the Bee Gees real centre of interest lay, in the creation of magical sound panoramas, of feeling, rather than profound lyrical perfection.

On the fumes of the success of 'How Can You Mend a Broken Heart', and with some arm-bending of sceptical Australian promoters, the Bee Gees arrived in Australia in July with a 16-piece orchestra for concerts in all the capital cities. Australia, where their Best of The Bee Gees compilation album from the previous year was to nestle at No. 5, forgot any historic slights and took them back as though they were prodigal sons; and that was where they received their gold albums for the compilation.

Unlike the Americans, the Australians flocked to the shows and filled the venues making the tills ring merrily. 15 of the best songs including 'Massachusetts', 'To Love Somebody' and 'I Started a Joke' drew screams from female fans with Barry as Heartthrob-in-Chief. There were long, standing ovations at the end of the concerts and shouts for more, whilst in Melbourne, demand was so great that another concert was arranged to cope with the numbers. The Bee Gees sound, rotating somewhat dazed between the charmed 60s and the brasher 70s, was still able to transport the faithful.

Now more diplomatic and mature, Barry would claim that they had two homes, Australia, which they "loved", and the UK. Australia, he said, would see them again before too long.

Nonetheless, the signs that the Bee Gees' popularity was fraying at the edges were unmistakable; one glance at the charts would show even them that trouble was brewing.

September saw the release of Trafalgar, their ninth album, which they'd finished recording in April of that year and which managed to limp up to No. 34 in the US. 'Don't Wanna Live Inside Myself' was the second single release and it fared even worse than the album, despite the promotional US tour in the autumn that also had them playing seven nights in New York. Neither album nor single charted in the UK.

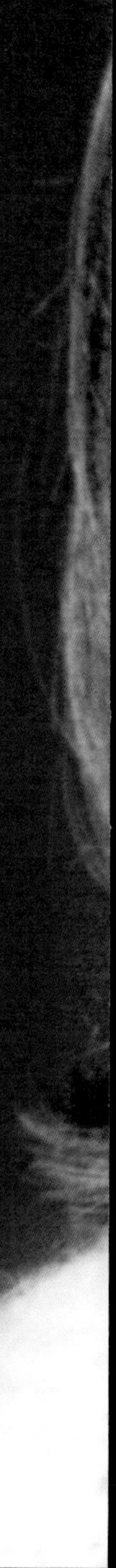

MAIN IMAGE:
Maurice Gibb following the shearing of his trademark beard, February 2nd 1970

EARLY SEVENTIES MEMORABILIA

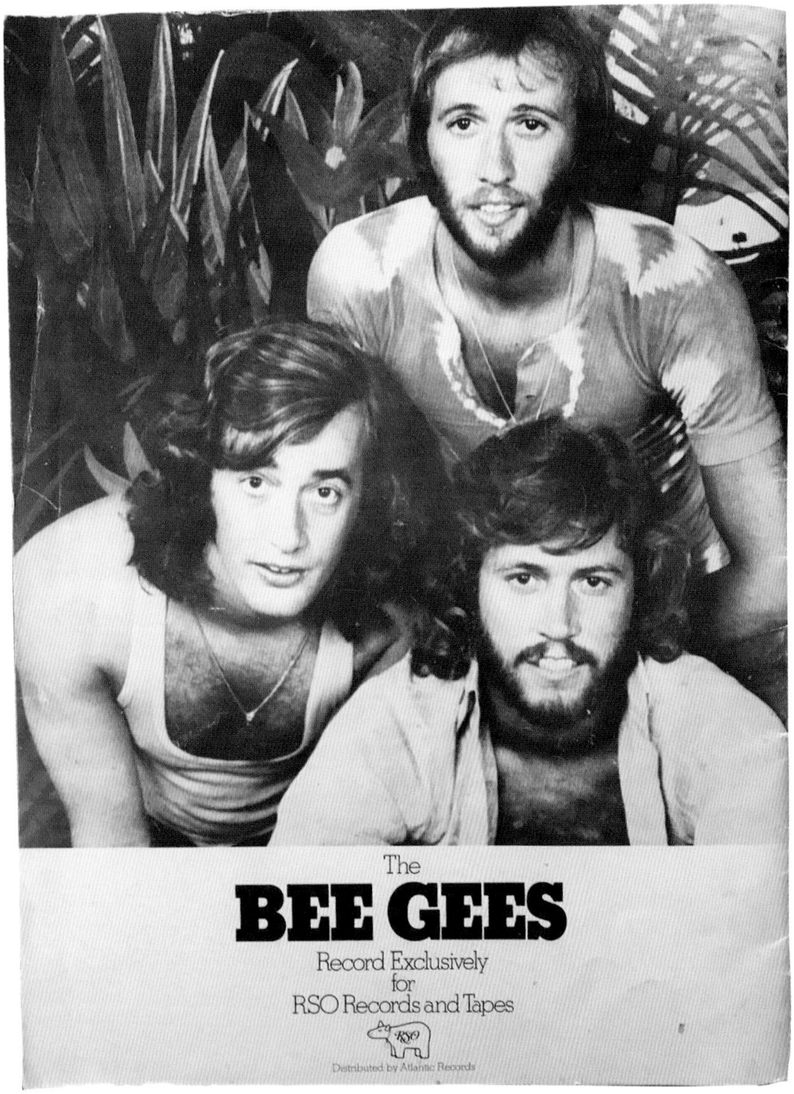

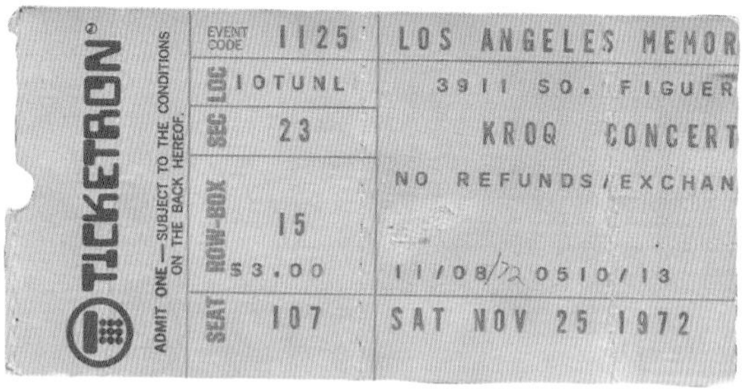

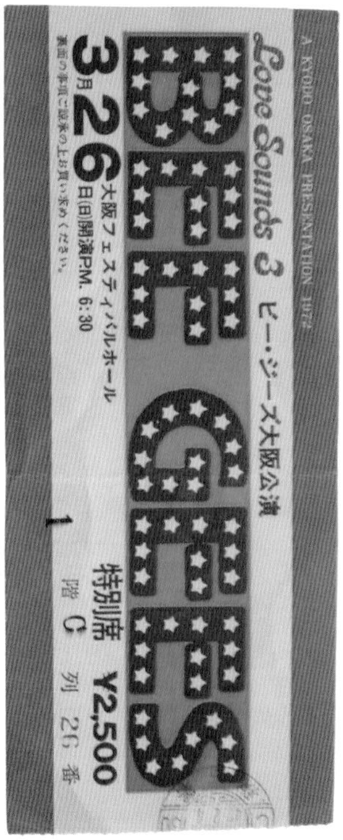

21st February, 1970
Australia 15c; New Zealand 15c; Rhodesia 2/-; West Africa 1/6; East Africa 2s.00; South Africa 15c; Malaysia 75c; Malta 1/4; Sverige SKr. 1.50 inkl moms; Deutschland Dm 1.00; Norge Kr. 2.40; Nederland Fl. 1.05; Danmark Kr. 2.60; Finland Fm. 1.20; Canada 35c; U.S.A. 35c; Italia 300 lire
1/-
Fabulous 208
They've got that loving feeling
New Love Affair
in double page colour
Steve Ellis
in kingsize colour
The Arrival arrive!
Your fave DJs choose what girls wear!
Radio Luxembourg programmes 17th–23rd February

1972
Bee Gees
A KYODO TOKYO PRESENTATION
BY ARRANGEMENT WITH ROBERT STIGWOOD, PAUL DAINTY / WATSON TAY

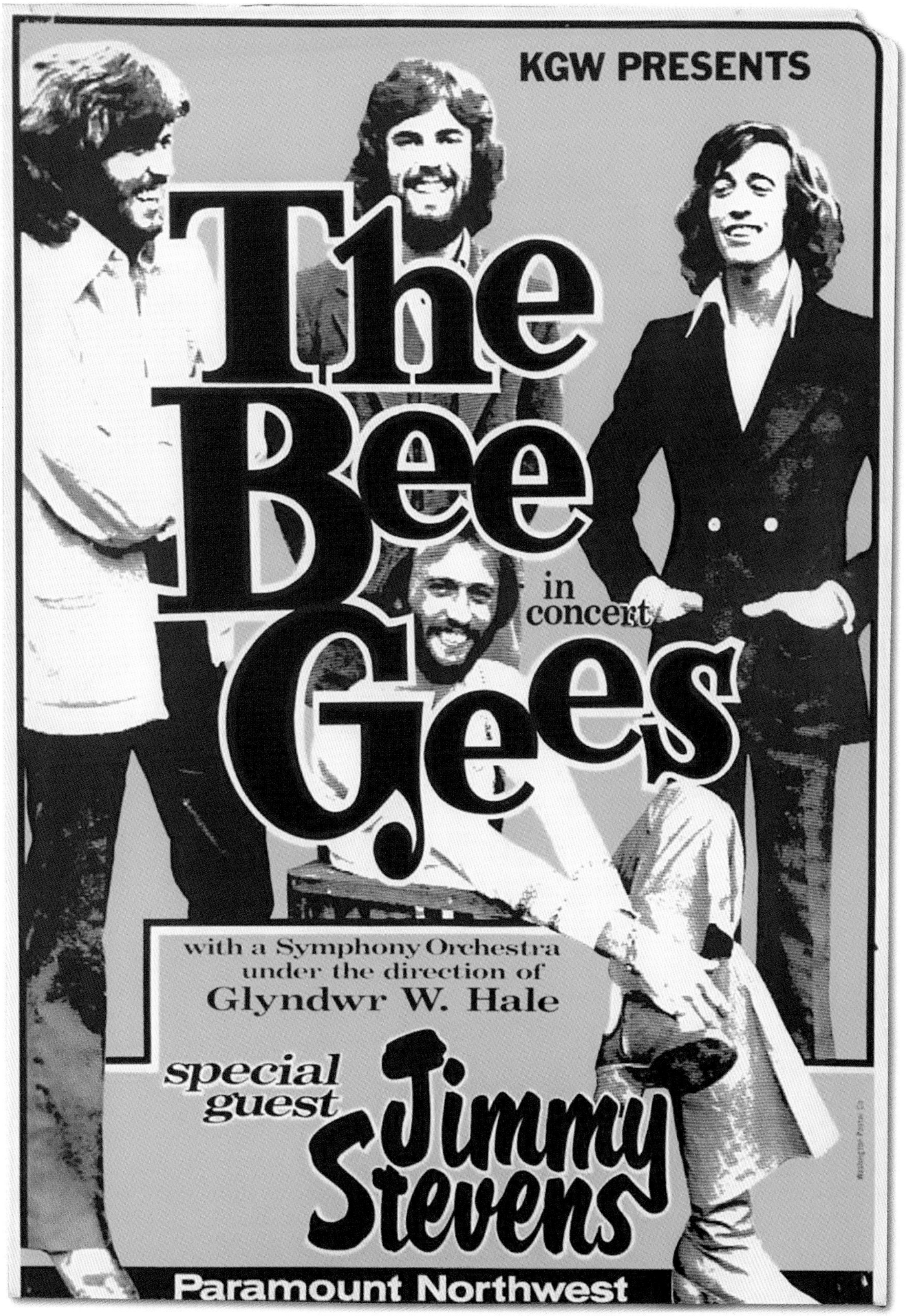
KGW PRESENTS
The Bee Gees
in concert
with a Symphony Orchestra
under the direction of
Glyndwr W. Hale
special guest
Jimmy Stevens
Paramount Northwest

POP WILDERNESS

Those singer songwriters and the edgy David Bowie were taking music in a new direction, making the Bee Gees seem old hat as they leant back on what they knew, the sumptuous orchestrations and heart-tugging emotional appeals from the lost boys that had served them so well, as epitomised in the melancholic 'Walking Back to Waterloo' from the Trafalgar album. Not even their first Grammy Award for 'How Can You Mend a Broken Heart' as Best Pop Performance by a Duo or Group with Vocals, nor watching 'My World' climb to No. 16 in both the UK and the US and 'Run to Me' break the top ten in the UK, could disguise the changing direction of the musical winds. There were live performances, too, such as the one at the Woodstock of the West festival in Los Angeles. But there would be no Bee Gees' soul-searching à la James Taylor; that was not their forte. There was, perhaps, too much and simultaneously too little in the psychological cooking pot and it was easier to examine one head than three.

The boys knew they were on borrowed time. Maurice's own marriage to Lulu was on the rocks and sinking fast, and he claimed that he had spent most of his money. He returned to the solace of The Isle of Man and the scenes of his childhood, joining young teenage brother Andy, who was living with Hugh and Barbara, who were now running a branch of the post office. Maurice took up residence in a small townhouse in an apparent confirmation of his impending poverty, and drove Andy to school. Until he was forced to sell the car. And he drank even more. What else was there to do with no parties to go to?

Barry, too, went back to the island leaving Robin alone on the mainland. His existential worries followed him, and he was now convinced that the Bee Gees were about to crash into the buffers unless they could wrench the wheel around and find new, innovative musical inspiration.

They had been recording in the studio earlier in the year for another bite at the cherry; To Whom it May Concern was an unfortunate name as upon its release in October 1972, it didn't seem to concern anyone in the US very much, where it peaked at number 35, doing rather better in Spain and Italy. It was the last vestige of the Bee Gees of old, continuing the tradition of Trafalgar. Guitarist Alan Kendall, who would line up beside them for another two decades, was in the lineup once more having made his debut with them on the Trafalgar album. Reviews were lukewarm. This was an album that was full of contrast and melodic variety, the tracks easy to listen to as they swayed between genre influences from country to Beatles.

It was a final wave to the past, leaving a hiatus that would eventually lead to an astonishing revival.

Before To Whom was released, they had adjourned to the Record Plant in Los Angeles to record the next offering. Life in a Tin Can was another of those titles that encapsulated the group's situation. Robin's son, Spencer, arrived during the sessions, and the album was released in January 1973 in the US and one month later in the UK.

Studio work had produced another new album by late 1972. It had been given a working title, which, if even no one knew what it meant, seemed to epitomise the brothers' fall from grace and descent into confusion; A Kick in the Head is Worth Eight in the Pants. Say no more. Originally it had been named The Bee Gees Album. As though no one could be bothered to think of a more inspiring title. Stigwood saw his worst fears confirmed when he heard it, a dead parrot of an album unworthy of them, he thought, before tactfully adding that it was not commercial enough. Some of the songs would resurface in later years. But as far as rock bottoms go, this one was pretty rocky.

But as 1972 eased into 1973, the decline became more

RIGHT:
Bee Gees portrait,October 22, 1972 in LA, California

introduction for the future as a motivation.

There were personal strains, too. By 1973, Lulu and Maurice had run their course as man and wife. Career pressures and alcohol finally succeeded in putting the boot into their marriage.

Lulu confessed that, as Barry had suspected, she had, indeed, been too young, too inexperienced, too in love with love, to really know what she was about to encounter in her partner. And even though she adored Maurice, the demon drink would beat her away as it had beaten down many other partnerships in the past. "We didn't have any responsibilities, we'd just party" Maurice commented.

They had both been child stars. "We'd felt a very strong connection" she said later, but admitted that they had lived a life removed from reality. "I decided it had to end. He didn't want it to end and it hurt him."

Life in a Tin Can, a pop rock, acoustic rock, folk-rock amalgam, was given the last rites by Rolling Stone magazine. "Recently, however" the reviewer wrote, having bemoaned the demise of their earlier "arresting" singles, "the melodies and harmonies have become drab and sparse, the arrangements correspondingly lusher (the lyrics became tame long ago). And Robin's throbbing histrionics now seem at odds with the group's currently trivial and simplistic repertoire". That hurt. A review seemingly at odds with the Album of the Year award the album attracted from Record World magazine. Rolling Stone did praise two tracks. 'Method to My Madness' for its "unadorned organ-dominated arrangement and slightly above-average melody", and also 'Saw a New Morning', made worthy thanks to its strong harmonies and rather complex structure. With sales of just 135,000 worldwide and no chart placing in the UK, however, it seems Rolling Stone was the more accurate compass needle.

The Bee Gees went out on tour with Life in a Tin Can, supported by their old friends the band Tin Tin, and during the course of the year, starting in February at the Royal

marked still. Even Stigwood had lost interest, his attention focussed on Eric Clapton or the film version of Jesus Christ Superstar, a huge money-spinner for RSO.

Whilst his brothers watched their careers nose dive, brother Andy, back on the Isle of Man, having decided to form a pop group to lessen the loneliness caused the absences of his famous brothers, was obviously as talented a singer as they were. And he'd been singing since he was 13. With billing making no mistake about who he was, he headed a band called Melody Fayre, and with a bass player, drummer and guitarist on board, played in local clubs and pubs. His brothers were enthusiastic, and Barry suggested he take himself off to Australia to get his career on the road and dangled a Stigwood

Festival Hall in London, visited Canada and the US as well Japan, hoping the venues would be fuller than the almost empty ones they had played to the previous year on the To Whom it May Concern tour.

Even a Best of Bee Gees Volume 2 couldn't save 1973 from joining in the slide. The Best of didn't chart in the UK and slunk up to 98 in the US. Despite the Bee Gees being invited to play alongside Chuck Berry, 1973 was not a year to remember fondly.

Nor, it seemed, would 1974 do them any favours in the popularity stakes. In fact, if there had been a time for them to disband, it might have happened round about then.

Instead, something else happened.

The brothers couldn't see their way out of the thicket they had built around themselves, but Barry was more than ready to accept advice on a change in direction. Arif Mardin offered that advice. Arif Mardin was a soul man.

Mr. Natural, was album number 10, and one that edged the boys towards funk, R&B and soul thanks to Arif. Turkish-born Berkley College graduate Mardin had founded Atlantic Records with his brother Ahmet, a label that in the 70s was producing the greatest of the great and good; Tom Waits, The Eagles, Roberta Flack. And having steered the careers of such greats as Carly Simon and Diana Ross, amongst others, he arrived inconspicuously in the Bee Gees' lives, and would be the one man credited with dragging them half-drowned from the waters of Mordor. Stigwood had organised a meeting with the Atlantic man, who brought the brothers into the Atlantic studios in New York, where they worked on new material from mid-November 1973 until late January 1974.

Producer, arranger and composer, Arif began to mould and nudge the Bee Gees' songs towards R&B. Maurice was relieved of the keyboards by Geoff Westley (and soon after by ex-Strawbs keyboardist Derek Weaver), and would now play just bass and sing backing vocals. Most of the songs were penned by Barry and Robin only, Maurice doing little writing in that year when his alcohol problems began to make themselves truly felt.

Nonetheless, during this trial period, they felt they still lacked a clear musical direction, even though "Arif was brilliant, full of ideas", as Maurice recalled, although Mo was dissatisfied with the end result, considering it a total disaster that in hindsight resembled a rehearsal for what was to come. Indeed, for the discerning ear, the Barry falsetto on 'Dogs' was just that.

In New York, they recorded 'Give a Hand, Take a Hand' and 'Lost in Your Love'; a harder rock sound, 'Heavy Breathing', and 'I Can't Let You Go' were from Los Angeles, whilst 'Mr. Natural' and 'Had a Lot of Love Last Night' were recorded in London's Command Studios.

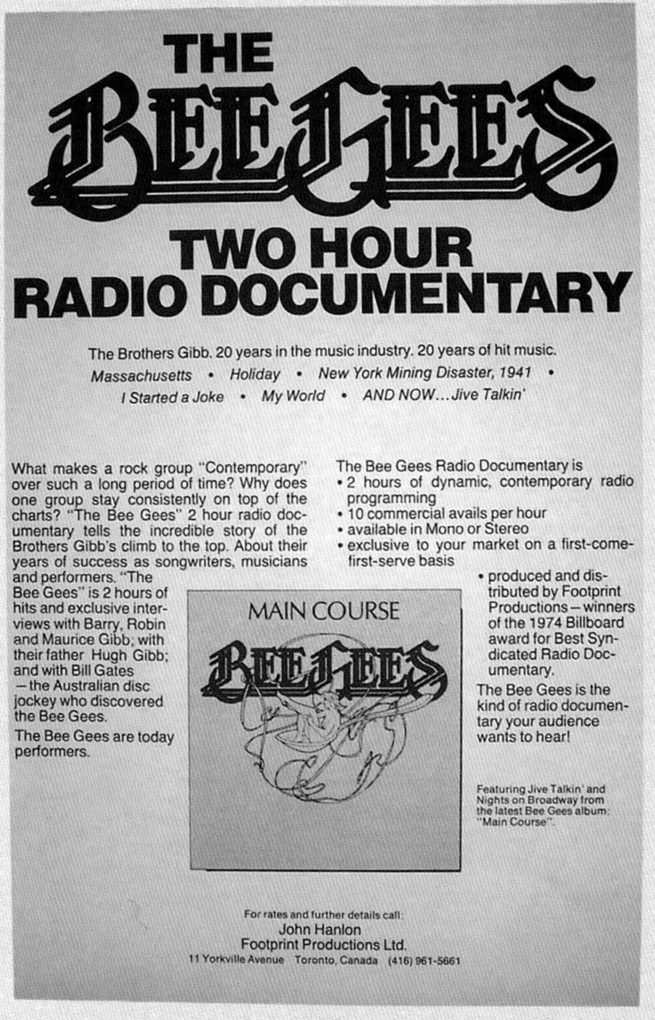

Mr. Natural was an attempt to produce a new sound. When the album was released in June of 1974, therefore, hopes were high that this experiment in upgrading the Bee Gees would point the way forward. It "injects new life into what could easily have become a moribund institution" said Rolling Stone astutely, whilst cautioning that "The slushy opener, 'Charade', proves the Bee Gees can still cook up a monumental turkey". Not exactly fulminant praise; and no praise came from any other quarter, the album failing to chart anywhere except faithful Australia at 20, and finding an embarrassing 178 in the US. This surely was the death knell.

Not if Arif had anything to do with it wasn't. It was a good start, he encouraged the boys, and they needed all the encouragement they could get at that point.

So they took off to tour the US and Canada before the UK, where they ended up playing to a few hundred souls in West Yorkshire's Batley Variety Club - to say it was a come down is an understatement, even though the club could boast that it had hosted some of the world's greatest stars from Louis Armstrong to Shirley Bassey, Roy Orbison and Neil Sedaka.

Batley was to prod itself into the Bee Gees' life in a significantly more romantic way, though, because a certain waitress by the name of Yvonne Spenceley was working there and did not escape the appreciative eyes of Maurice.

Maurice hadn't intended to remarry, but with Yvonne, he knew he had found the right one. They would have two children, Adam Andrew born on the 23rd of February 1976 and Samantha Amanda on the 2nd of July 1980, and Maurice and Yvonne would remain a couple despite his drinking problems, until his death.

His memory of the first moment was, "I just saw her eyes and said to myself, 'This is the woman I'm going to marry' ".

RIGHT:
Bee Gees group portrait, Windsor, UK, 1974

Yvonne received an offer that was too great to ignore, and she handed in her notice one week later. She was going to tour with the Bee Gees.

And so was brother Andy, a huge fillip to his fledgling career. There were plans for a recording session with Melody Fayre, and they recorded 'To a Girl' in September, Maurice lending his vocal backing, though the single never saw the light of day. Andy's other 6 tracks fared better.

His face seemed to be omnipresent, although most of the time he and the band were fancy free in Australia; a state of stasis. Andy enjoyed the financial support and generosity of his famous brothers, which meant he didn't need to sing for his supper. So he would adjourn to the beach or vanish at various times, leaving his backup musicians Alderson and Stringer without any gig work and therefore without income, forcing them to work in burger joints. This unsustainable and miserable situation eventually led to the band splitting the following year with Alderson and Stringer returning home. Whereupon Andy joined forces with the band Zenta.

So as the Australian tour got underway in late 1974, and it delivered the boys the shot in the arm they needed so badly. As the lights picked them out on stage in Melbourne, Barry looking radiant in red pants and Robin and Barry gleaming and slick, the audience hit the roof. England might be abandoning them but OZ was glad to see them. Their performances showed partly, perhaps, what was going wrong with their approach. Their mixture of old and new songs was family fun, they bowed formally between songs and left nothing to that card shark known as spontaneity.

But the audiences were ecstatic, and the shows sold out just as they once used to.

GOLD CHAINS AND PLATFORM SHOES

With little to sustain their hopes as they entered the new year of 1975, the boys took up a suggestion from Eric Clapton to record in Miami, where he had relaunched his career after his successful battle against drug addiction, in the warmth and creative atmosphere of an area he loved.

The sunshine must have raised the brothers' spirits a little, and Mardin had flown in, too, armed with more musicians; keyboard player 'Blue' Weaver amongst them. No one could have had an inkling of the extraordinary turn around in fortunes that was going to happen in a very short space of time and change not only the boys' lives but the course of pop music history.

No time was lost in Miami, and recording started on the 6th of January.

Despite the change of atmosphere, they started off by falling back onto their tried and tested ballads, yet again ignoring the hard facts they should have been confronting; hardly a revolution in the making. And not what Arif and Stigwood had in mind. Stigwood stepped in to suggest that perhaps they might think of heading in the direction of the music trend of the moment; disco. Even a few years later they had difficulty accepting that they had ever been writing anything else; Robin commented, We were always writing the kind of music we do now, but we weren't putting it down right. We were writing R&B, but we weren't going in an R&B direction".

So, no change of direction, just an adjustment in style.

By 1975, disco, born of the black, Puerto Rican and gay discotheques and underground dance scene in New York, was rapidly displacing rock and singer songwriters from the record-buying consciousness, and Miami was an epicentre of the genre; with its absorption of all things Latin American, it was hardly surprising that infectious dance rhythms would eventually break out there. However, disco's provenance gave it an identity problem in the white conservative heartland of the US.

There were clubs in town such as the 1235 club that were the places to go, where money and drugs were on show, where the sound was eardrum-rupturing and the vibe electric. This was the mood that the Bee Gees needed to tap into, and they were in the centre of the whirlpool with the rewards there for the taking. Their Road to Damascus moment took a while; it was the end of January already as they drove across town to the studio. The car was trying to tell them something. As it rattled over the road surface on a bridge, it beat out a rhythm that one of them finally heard, and picking up the beat, they immediately wrote a song to match it; their speedwriting talents had come to their rescue.

'Drive Talkin' ' was played to Arif, who immediately asked them if they knew what Jive Talkin' meant. The boys though it meant you were dancing. It wasn't, Arif informed them, it meant they were bull...ing. The title was changed, the lyrics, too, and the Bee Gees were reborn. Arif took the song and worked his magic, Maurice agreed, "setting the groove, the tempo, everything" besides offering one of his most valuable pieces of advice. "Take it up an octave", he said to Barry.

Of course, this adopting of black culture would lay them open to accusations of cultural appropriation. But with their British sensibilities not attuned to those of American racial

RIGHT:
The Bee Gees in Amsterdam, 1975

tensions, as far as the Bee Gees were concerned, as Robin pointed out, "We didn't think that there were any 'no go' areas; it's music!" So three Englishmen in a bind blithely sailed into the black world and reinvented themselves in doing so.

With Maurice's bass rasping to reproduce the sound of the serendipitous car beat, the drums seductively pumping out the funky rhythms and Blue Weaver's keyboard expressing the pure joy of movement, the Bee Gees had been transformed with a little help from their canny friends. Stigwood, had contributed, too. Robin confirmed it; "Robert has this thing about songs that break up in the middle with a slow piece". Unlike other band gurus, however, Stigwood had no wish to plant his flag on any part of the creative process. "I can't claim any contribution to their songwriting. I wish I could. I'd be taking their royalties, I assure you".

Thus was 'Jive Talking' composed, and the rest is... well, disco.

There was another new Bee Gees sound about to emerge from these sessions, this time from Barry.

Barry was no stranger to the falsetto sound he could produce, but this time he was challenged to produce it for longer and with lyrics. When he tried it, those listening in the control room were ecstatic. So he attempted 'Final Nights on Broadway' and from then on would compose

SCANDIN

songs that incorporated his unique vocal contribution. It would make the Bee Gees stand out from the crowd, helping to propel them to superstardom.

For a band that had not hit the US top ten since 1970 and 'How Can You Mend a Broken Heart', there was a lot riding on this album. It was released in June 1975 as The Main Course. It was preceded by the single 'Jive Talkin' '. The single's plain white cover without any reference to the Bee Gees, was a canny marketing ploy to get DJs to break the association of Bee Gees and a band that had faded. It worked superbly. A DJ had no idea whose record he was playing until he had the needle in the groove.

With stunned reactions when it was discovered that this sharp new sound emanated from the Bee Gees, the single 'Jive Talkin' ' began it's rise to domination. Within two months of its release in May, it had struck gold status, and one month later was on the number one spot in the US, as well as hitting No. 5 in the UK. As AllMusic magazine reported later, "the writing was simpler, and the rest of (the album) was made up of catchy dance tunes (heavily influenced by the Philadelphia-based soul music of the period) in which the beat and the texture of the voices and instruments took precedence over the words. The

Indeed it did.

It would be another few years before the band achieved a No. 1 in the States, though.

The Main Course, considered now as the Bee Gees' comeback album, reached No. 14 on the US Billboard chart in 1975, but hovered for 74 weeks on the Billboard Top 200 albums chart. 'Nights on Broadway' and 'Fanny (Be Tender With My Love)', also slipped into the US top ten. 'Country Lanes' and 'Come on Over' were awkward throwbacks to pre-disco Bee Gees, though 'Come on Over' did hit No. 1 on the US Billboard Easy Listening chart.

Critical acclaim was widespread, some of it grudging and

MAIN IMAGE:
The Bee Gees in Denmark, 1975

petty, but everyone acknowledged that the group had come good. They appeared on Midnight Special that year to promote the album, singing a medley of songs and sending fans into raptures at the superb harmonic beauty of the voices.

The newspapers were all buzzing again later that year when Maurice crowned a year of superlatives with his marriage to Yvonne Spenceley, on the 17th of October 1975 in Hayward's Heath.

December brought less welcome news to the brothers. Robert Stigwood decided to change his business relationships in America and use Polygram instead of Atlantic. The change was the death knell of the relationship between Mardin Arif, the man who had engineered the Bee Gees' revival, and the three brothers. The timing could not have been worse, for they needed to prove that The Main Course was not a flash in the pan, and with Mardin by their side they had felt that success would be almost guaranteed.

A new producer was quickly brought in, Richard Perry, who had worked with such greats as Barbra Streisand and Carly Simon. The association was short lived, lasting three days, in fact, before they parted company. Perry had rejected a song, 'You Should Be Dancing'. A bad move, as the phenomenal success of the single would prove. And how fortunate that the Bee Gees still believed in themselves strongly enough to go their own way. Deciding that Barry should become producer, the boys continued recording, Barry was assisted by Karl Richardson, the engineer who

ABOVE:
The Bee Gees in the recording studio, 1975

had worked with Mardin, and a musical advisor in the shape of Albhy Galuten, who had worked on The Main Course album.

In fact, the new album, Children of the World, would produce a string of hits apart from 'You Should Be Dancing', which brought them a No. 1 in the US. 'Love So Right', 'You Stepped Into My Life' and 'Boogie Child' all followed one another to the upper echelons of the charts. The Bee Gees may have lost some fans, but along the way they had gained a whole new following.

Andy, back in Australia, was not having the luck to experience a revival of his career. His brothers's success seemed to heighten his own lack of it, despite a new band, Zenta and an appearance on a high-rating TV show, Countdown. His music, like that of his brothers before him, had become stuck in a middle-of-the-road rut.

But as the new year of 1976 dawned, Stigwood, who had heard some of the younger Gibb's demos and knew a potential star when he heard one, signed Andy to his own label. It helped having brother Barry on his side. "I want to produce you" Barry had told Andy, "Stigwood wants to manage you." So fired with ambition was Andy that he left Zenta, and Australia, without even telling his band.

In Miami Beach, Florida, again with the help of his brother Barry, and Albhy Galuten (who helped write two songs on the new album, 'Dance to the Light of the Morning' and 'Too Many Looks in Your Eyes') as producer, he started working on new songs before going to the Criteria Studios towards the end of the year to start the sessions for his first album, which was to be called Flowing Rivers.

By then, he had married his girlfriend, Kim Reeder. Once again, history repeated itself in the Gibb family, as Barry raised objections that Andy at 18 was too young; both Barry and Mo had been in that position. But Andy would not be budged, and the lovers tied the knot on July the 11th, 1976 in Sydney. (Barry was proven right again. Andy and Kim had a daughter, Peta, but divorced in 1978, the year that she was born.)

Barry, seemed to have the energy of two, for that same year when the wave began to break over the Bee Gees, he was in the studio working with Andy, and on one occasion bringing in The Eagles' guitarist with the badman reputation, Joe Walsh, for two tracks. Barry co-wrote two songs, '(Love is) Thicker Than Water' and 'I Just Want to be Your Everything', both important songs for the album. But Andy was flying high writing all but two of the songs on the album himself.

Andy had to prove to himself and the world that he wasn't just riding on his famous brothers' coat tails but a star in his own right. As teen idol material, he had the luck of history on his side, for the teen idol was back in vogue, and with his fresh-faced good looks, he was in the right place at the right time. And it was encouraging that the first single from his album, 'I Just Want to Be Your Everything', written by Barry, who was also the backup vocalist, zipped up to number one in the US, Australian and Canadian charts and became the most played record of the year.

Andy had become a success overnight, separate from his brothers yet part of them in style, thanks to one single and his smooth good looks; but he never forgot who had helped him to get there. Barry, had "steered" his career, he admitted later, and it was "chiefly to my brother Barry" that he believed he owed his career.

The younger Gibb became a TV chat show regular, and although he hated it, he could never escape the references to his brothers, never forget that he and they were bound in blood and music. It was, perhaps, a fatal flaw in the equation, for Andy would flounder around in the doubt that it was his own talent as a skilled guitarist, singer and songwriter that had brought him success and not the ineluctable suction from his older brothers' fame. At every opportunity, he would express his desire to stand as an artist in his own right. With his single high up on the peak, Andy was experiencing a dangerous rocket ride to fame. His angelic appearance was mesmerising to anyone watching him on stage or TV, and the likeness to Barry was unmistakable. Unlike his older brother, sadly, he would not escape the demons lurking in the dark.

For behind the glittering scenes designed for public consumption, reality was proving a hard taskmaster.

In LA, Andy's new money and celebrity status secured entry to the elite establishments, and he took to the high life like a true Gibb. Partying, playing and indulging in drugs and excess, he received a warning from Kim to get his life back in order; and when he refused to haul in the horses, she wisely took her pregnant self off back to Australia, where she gave birth to Peta. It was clear that Barry's words had been prophetic. The marriage was rapidly heading for the waterfall.
Although Andy had promised that he would return for the birth, the seduction of glittering parties in America proved to be too great. Kim only learned that she was to be divorced when she opened a Sydney newspaper. Two weeks later, she went into labour for 40 hours. It was all too much for Kim who almost had a nervous breakdown, and her weight plummeted to 45 kg.

In the heady atmosphere of privilege, Andy would not remain alone for long, and a string of famous girls were soon seen with him, including Marie Osmond and British actress Susan George, eight years his senior. He reported that he was "close to being in love" with her.

While Andy would soon discover the joys and horrors delivered with the great quantities of cocaine that wealth could buy, his brothers were succumbing to their demons in different ways.

Mo had been introduced to his favourite drink, scotch and coke, by John Lennon; "If he had given me cyanide, I would have drunk the cyanide, I was so in awe of the man" he said later. Now, the addiction to alcohol was proving hard to shake off, and he was even arrested at home in the Isle of Man for driving on the pavement – he was also wearing an American policeman's uniform at the time; he'd become an avid collector of police paraphernalia.

At the same time, Robin was struggling with amphetamines, which suppressed his appetite and almost cost him his sanity. In the grip of paranoia, he would be unable to disembark from planes, even if there were no fans waiting, and even if no crush barriers had been erected. Robin was by far "the most eccentric of the three", mused Chris Hutchins, one of Robin's former PR men.

AllMusic's retrospective review on Children of the World found the group "in very good form" and praised the album as beautifully sung, noting that Barry had now taken over as obvious lead singer with Robin and Maurice relegated from the centre stage and Barry's falsetto singing dominating the ensemble. And it was "one of the most enjoyably lighthearted albums" that the group was to produce.

Rolling Stone was less happy. While gushing that 'You Should Be Dancing' was a killer single, the reviewer felt that it seemed to have "left most of the rest of the album listing aimlessly", and he delivered the coup de grâce with "the current record's only saving grace is a whiny soul falsetto, somewhere between Tony Washington of the Dynamic Superiors and the Stylistics' Russell Tompkins".

The lads had succeeded in distancing themselves from their past musical iteration by trying to create what Mardin would have produced, and they succeeded brilliantly, creating delicious ballads and disco pure. They were ecstatic to be back on top again; somewhat amazed at their revival and completely unaware that the pinnacle had not yet been reached. But then, who could have imagined what was waiting around the next bend in the musical road.

RIGHT:
Andy Gibb performing in 1977

LATE SEVENTIES MEMORABILIA

BEE GEES
TM
©1979 Bee Gees

BEE GEES
1979 TOUR

BEE GEES
1979 TOUR
Bob Sherman

A SEVERE CASE OF NIGHT FEVER

What follows should really be the Robert Stigwood story, for it was the producer, who, following his instinct for the right material at the right time, had read a story by an Englishman named Nick Cohen and sniffed the sweet scent of success. The article was about a young, 18-year old boy, who would don his disco gear, flares and all, for his one chance to shine in an otherwise ordinary week; at the weekend disco in his local club. Stigwood, enthused by the success of his Jesus Christ Superstar film, bought the rights to the story, which became the central plot in another film Stigwood planned to produce, which bore the title Saturday Night.

Ironically, the story, Tribal Rights of the New Saturday Night, which was published in the New York Times, turned out to be a fabrication spun by Cohen, who was at a loss to understand the American subculture he had been asked to write about. So he chose a subculture he did know about, the British mods, and chose a friend of his as his central character.

Stigwood and screenwriter Norman Wexler got to work creating the dance film concept and gave the lead role, Tony Manero, to John Travolta, thus changing the actor's life forever in the process, and casting Karen Lynn Gorney as his dance partner. Even Travolta's mother and sister had bit parts in the film.

Production was well underway when Stigwood followed up on another idea that had occurred to him and made a phone call that would change three other lives as well.

"We're putting together this little film, low budget, called Tribal Rites of a Saturday Night. Would you have any songs on hand?" he asked the Gibbs over the phone.
The Gibb brothers were ensconced in a French studio working on a live album, having recently finished a tour, when Stigwood paid them a visit to pitch the idea of a working class kid earning his living in a paint store in New York and strutting his stuff in a disco at night. It didn't strike a chord immediately. But Stigwood hadn't got where he was by being a pushover, and he then asked the boys if they had any new songs that might suit. As it happened, they said, yes they did, because if the world wanted disco, then with Barry now the obvious leader of the group, disco is what the world would get in spades. They were working on 'Stayin' Alive', 'More Than a Woman' and 'How Deep is Your Love', a gift from heaven for Stigwood. Encouraged, Stigwood wanted a title song from them, and while feeling that Night Fever would be too pornographic, the suggestion was soon incorporated into the title track for a film that would conquer the world; Saturday Night Fever, and from part of its legendary and hugely successful soundtrack.

The Bee Gees were writing blind, as it were, with no idea where and how their songs would be placed in the film, or even what the film was about, and during filming, Travolta danced to substitute music from artists such as Stevie Wonder as the Bee Gees' songs weren't ready.

Rolling Stone magazine reported Barry recalling Stigwood's words: "Give me eight minutes; eight minutes, three moods. I want frenzy at the beginning. Then I want some passion. And then I want some wiiilld frenzy!" The result was 'Stayin' Alive', composed in just two hours.

Stigwood was stunned by their writing abilities that saw four songs composed in a week.

"It's obviously easy. We did it" was Robin's laconic comment. They did it in the same way that they always wrote; by sitting down together, bouncing lines between

themselves - nothing written down as they couldn't read or write musical notation, but retaining everything in their musical brains - and then recording. Thus they rattled off the biggest hits of their careers.

In fact, the boys would only see the end product of their efforts once the film hit the big screens, when they had Stigwood raise the volume of the music so that the dancers' feet hitting the floor couldn't be heard.

In all, the lads contributed eight tracks to the soundtrack, and their infectious beats took the film to a level of energy that made it special. Travolta as Tony swaggered through the film, his ego fed by the irresistible Bee Gees' rhythms.

The soundtrack was released in November 1977 and became the best-selling album of all time until Michael Jackson's Thriller arrived, selling from 175,000 to 200,000 copies each day, and striking the No. 1 spot in every major territory including the US, the UK, and Australia, of course. It hovered in the charts for over 2 years and has now sold over 40,000,000 copies, second only to Whitney Houston's Bodyguard at over 42,000,000.

(Incidentally, Michael Jackson acknowledged his debt to the Bee Gees, saying that their music had a big impact on his 1982 Thriller album, and he and the brothers, Barry in particular, became close, with Jackson occasionally taking refuge in Barry's house when the world got too loud.)

The soundtrack came out just ahead of the film (on the 16th of December, which opened to great reviews).

"Travolta does one solo ... that the audiences cheered for." The director John Badham's "camera occupies the dance floor so well that we really do understand the lure of the disco world, for all of the emptiness and cruelty the characters find there."

"... the music moves with a spring in it's step and the movie does, too", wrote another reviewer, acknowledging that

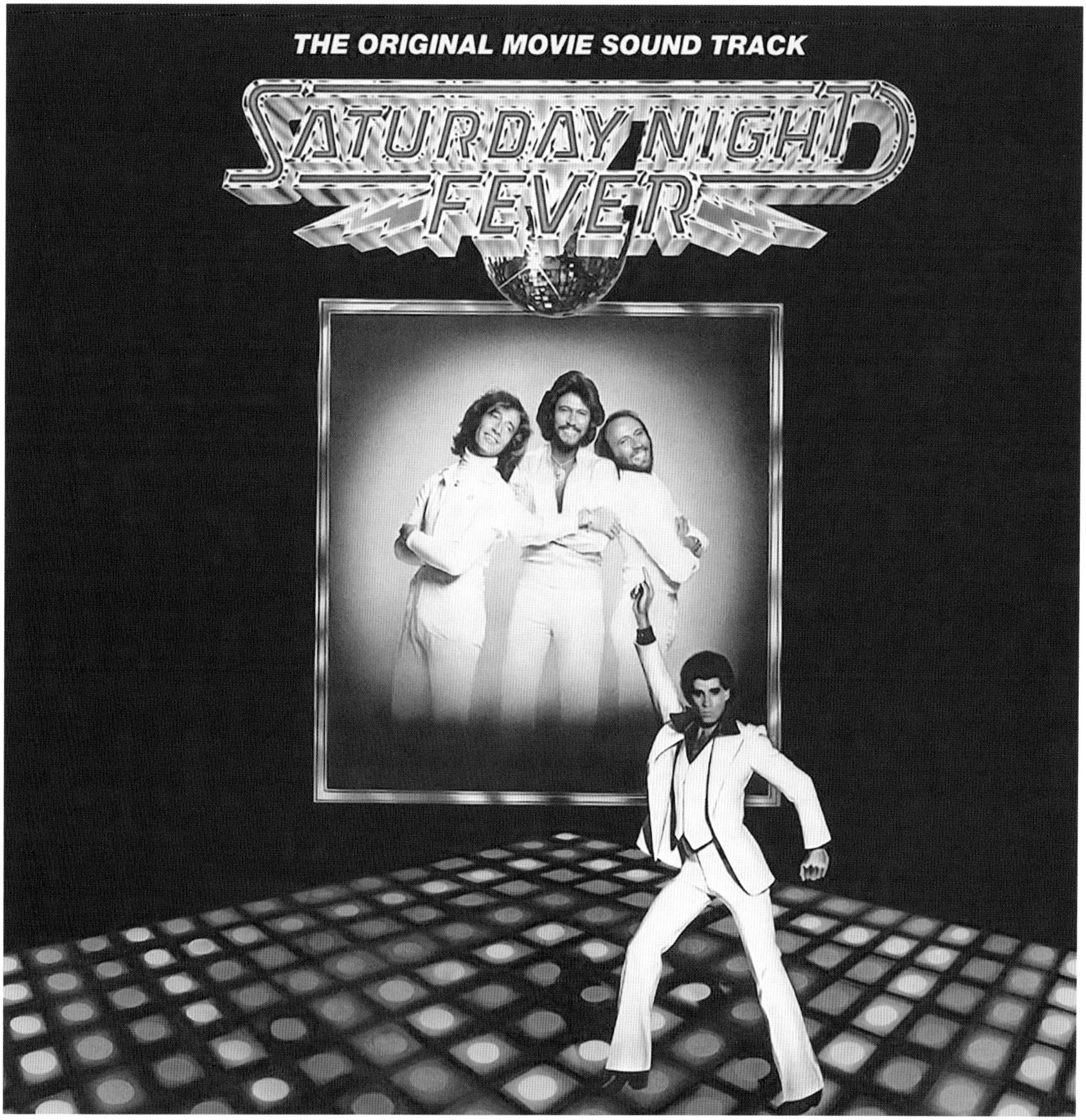

ABOVE:
Saturday Night Fever cover, 1977

LEFT:
Saturday Night Fever original movie poster, 1977

the Bee Gees wrote "the most important parts of (the film's) score".

Would the film have been as successful without the Bee Gees' contribution? Rotten Tomatoes was quick to credit the Bee Gees with enhancing the success; "Saturday Night Fever's huge success grew meteorically thanks to the towering popularity of its soundtrack". It then added that it was impossible to decipher whether "the hit movie was feeding the hit songs or the hit songs were feeding the hit movie".

Even today, the film is described not just as the disco film of the era, but as "a bracingly honest exploration of what it means to be young, horny, broke, and filled with intense feelings you can't express and don't understand".

The album won the Grammy Award for Album of the Year and was added to the National Recording Registry in the Library of Congress in America in 2013 to be preserved long term. It's cultural repercussions were huge, for the crossover between and within the music - it swayed from R&B to pop - and the film set the points for many future films and proved to be the demarcation line between the peak of 1970s disco culture and its decline. "Few soundtracks have defined a genre" enthused Rolling Stone. "This one did and more."

Despite the madness, the Bee Gees remained rooted in reality.

"We're fully aware that our music is almost totally commercial" Barry admitted. "We write for the present." Which they knew was the best way to tackle their lives, having been through a bust-up and hell and high water to keep themselves on track. They knew where their strengths lay and where they should not dare to tread.

Yet, opined Rolling Stone, "There was always something awkward about them, even when they were fresh and tender. They were rock stars, but they weren't really a rock band; they were a showbiz family in an age when rock was king"; middle of the road, and yet they drew comparisons

MAIN IMAGE:
Bee Gees, circa 1977

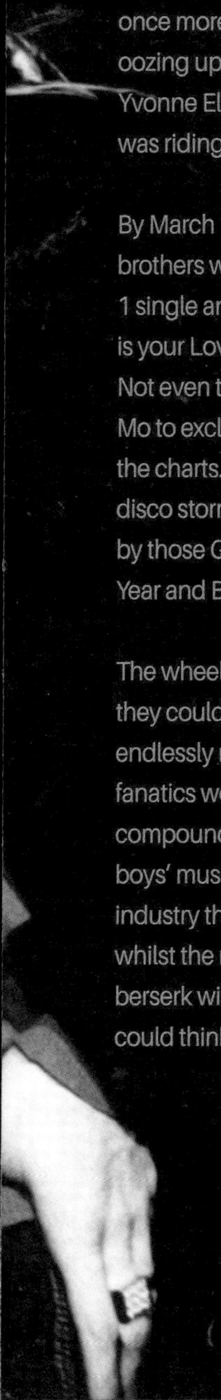

to the Beatles. Perhaps it was the tightness of their family ties that made them always seem perennially slightly out of sync with their surroundings.

They should have felt free to follow the new fashion trends of "white shirts and spiffy suits onstage" wrote Rolling Stone, but they stopped doing that. Barry's explanation was that "It's too hot up there".

Although they were older, "they're still natural, still innocents" the magazine went on, musing that perhaps that was why people liked them so much.

Suddenly, the Bee Gees were plastered all over the charts once more; 'Stayin' Alive' and 'More Than a Woman' were oozing upwards, and 'If I Can't Have You' covered by Yvonne Elliman was on its way to the top, too. Plus, Andy was riding high with Barry's 'Shadow Dancing'.

By March 1978, four songs written or performed by the brothers were the top four US singles. They had the No. 1 single and album in the US Billboard charts. 'How deep is your Love' stayed in the Australian charts for 31 weeks. Not even the Beatles had achieved such riches, leading Mo to exclaim, that they weren't in the charts, they were the charts. And they were the disco band, in the eye of the disco storm. And all this glory and adulation was topped off by those Grammys for Album of the Year, Producer of the Year and Best Pop Vocal (for 'How Deep is Your Love').

The wheel was spinning out of control; the boys felt that they couldn't breathe and certainly couldn't answer the endlessly ringing phone anymore. In Miami, fans and fanatics would attempt to get to the house, over the compound fence, whilst cars passed by and blasted the boys' music back at them at ear-splitting levels. The music industry that wasn't involved in the success was peeved, whilst the marketing men on the Bee Gees' side went berserk with every piece of marketing paraphernalia they could think of flooding the market bearing the visages of Barry, Mo, Robin and Andy. Every boy wanted to emulate them or Travolta in the myriad discos that burst open like blossoms, wearing platform shoes, flares, flower shirts open to the waist and golden jewellery, with the girls permed and dressed to up the nines.

Whilst Saturday Night Fever was raking in some $100,000,000 a year in 1978, Andy, too, was sailing into blue waters of his own, with his first three singles striking the gong at the top of the US charts, one after the other, making him the first solo artist in US chart history to achieve this three-card trick. 'Shadow Dancing' was the latest to climb the peak - and it turned out to be the last of its kind.

He knew he was on a short rein as a teen idol, though, and gave himself three to five years before that particular game finished, and was already thinking ahead to how he could keep the female fans on board as he grew older. Of more immediate concern to his ego, though, was the eternal nagging doubt; was he now an independently successful artist or still the younger brother to the Bee Gees, basking in reflected glory. And the doubt seemed justified. For although Andy was the flavour of the month, commanding a great enough draw to warrant an appearance on the Bob Hope Christmas Special that Christmas, his host felt compelled to ask him about his famous brothers.

In the public eye and consciousness, however, Andy was the golden boy in tight pants and open shirts who glittered alongside ABBA and Olivia Newton-John - now the hottest, curly haired, smiling cutie on the block since her appearance in Stigwood's other blockbuster, Grease - in an hour-long special on American TV. The TV audience did not hold back and screamed their adoration for the angelic young Gibb.

For the four Brothers Gibb, who had scaled the heights to musical superstardom, where else was there to go – except down.

MAIN IMAGE:
Bee Gees perform in New York, 1977

POST-FEVER BLUES

The Bee Gees seemed to have shadowed the Beatles all their careers and had admired and often been compared to them in earlier iterations of the Bee Gees setup. They'd even covered some of their songs, so it seemed a natural progression to be asked to appear in the Sgt. Pepper's Lonely Hearts Club Band film that would be shot in 1977 and early 1978; they accepted the challenge with glee. Especially as it was a Stigwood project; 29 Beatles' tracks with Peter Frampton thrown in for good measure.

This rock-opera-type story of a band, the Bee Gees, engaged in a fight against the music industry and the forces of evil attempting to steal their instruments and ruin the town of Heartland, whose mayor and the films' narrator was George Burns, was based on an off-Broadway production. The musical comedy, for the most part, featured Beatles' songs from Sgt. Pepper and Abbey Road.

Barry was flushed with enthusiasm, and a host of other stars, such as Steve Martin, Frankie Howerd (who praised the boys for their professionalism and lack of star attitude) and Donald Pleasance, also made the mistake of appearing in the film. It wasn't the best decision the band had ever made, as the 1978 Stinkers Bad Movie Awards testified. The film was nominated as the Worst Picture.

So what went wrong for the talented trio.

Well, musicians do not inevitably make good actors, although their fame might seduce them to believe in their own invincibility, and the Bee Gees were no exception. Miscast in the role of the Ersatz Beatles, their film careers, if they had ever existed independently of the Bee Gees biosphere, were killed stone dead and thrown to the vultures after this excursion.

Resentments bubbled up when it was revealed that they were earning in the region of one million for the film, whilst others, such as Alice Cooper, were pulling in much less. The whole blancmange, filled with thwarted suicide, death and restoration to life, and villains transformed into a monk and bishop, was given a finale that brought the stars of the film and a host of invited stars together - from Tina Turner to Carol Channing, Frankie Valli or Donovan and Helen Reddy - for the title track reprise, as a tribute to the Sgt. Pepper album cover. That finale cost an over-confident Stigwood more than $500, 000.

When Peter Frampton was involved in a car crash just before the film opened it seemed prophetic.

The film was released on the 21st of July 1978, and elicited spasms of bewildered horror and contempt amongst critics and public alike. Finding a good word about it was akin to searching for a needle in a field of haystacks. "Good, campy fun" was about as enthusiastic as anyone got.

Critic Leonard Maltin thought that "it ranges from tolerable to embarrassing". From the New York Times came, "... musical numbers are strung together so mindlessly that the movie has the feel of an interminable variety show... when whimsy gets to be this overbearing, it simply isn't whimsy any more".

As Classic Rock magazine astutely pointed out, "... both the Bee Gees and Frampton were caught up in a soulless music-industry machine - just like the one the movie's heroes fight against". And as history proved, the minnows who thought they were whales, lost the fight. The film was not only a critical and box-office disaster, it derailed the careers of Frampton and the Bee Gees.

Classic Rock magazine was not alone in its analysis; ex-Beatle George Harrison said of the film; "I think it's damaged their images, their careers, and they didn't need

RIGHT:
With Peter Frampton on the set of the film 'Sgt. Pepper's Lonely Hearts Club Band', LA, 1977

L'évènement "rock-musical" d'une génération
Sgt. Pepper's
Lonely Hearts Club Band
SOLD
PETER FRAMPTON
LES BEE GEES
"SGT. PEPPER'S LONELY HEARTS CLUB BAND"
FRANKIE HOWERD, PAUL NICHOLAS, DONALD PLEASENCE
et STEVE MARTIN
AEROSMITH · ALICE COOPER · EARTH, WIND & FIRE · BILLY PRESTON
et GEORGE BURNS
JOHN LENNON & PAUL McCARTNEY
GEORGE HARRISON

A Splendid Time Is Guaranteed For All*
A ROBERT STIGWOOD PRODUCTION
IN ASSOCIATION WITH DEE ANTHONY OF
A FILM BY MICHAEL SCHULTZ
PETER FRAMPTON
THE BEE GEES
Sgt. Pepper's Lonely Hearts Club Band
Starring FRANKIE HOWERD · PAUL NICHOLAS · DONALD PLEASENCE
Introducing SANDY FARINA as Strawberry Fields · DIANNE STEINBERG as Lucy
and STEVE MARTIN as Dr. Maxwell Edison
Special Guest Stars
AEROSMITH · ALICE COOPER · EARTH, WIND & FIRE · BILLY PRESTON
and GEORGE BURNS as Mr. Kite
Music and Lyrics by JOHN LENNON and PAUL McCARTNEY
"Here Comes The Sun" by GEORGE HARRISON
Director of Photography OWEN ROIZMAN ASC · Associate Producer BILL OAKES · Executive In Charge of Production ROGER M. ROTHSTEIN
Choreography by PATRICIA BIRCH · Music Arranged and Directed by GEORGE MARTIN · Written by HENRY EDWARDS
Executive Producer DEE ANTHONY · Produced by ROBERT STIGWOOD · Directed by MICHAEL SCHULTZ
RSO FILMS
ORIGINAL SOUNDTRACK ALBUM AVAILABLE ON RSO RECORDS AND TAPES
A UNIVERSAL PICTURE · TECHNICOLOR®
DOLBY STEREO
Now a POCKET BOOKS paperback
ONE SHEET "SGT. PEPPERS"

to do that. It's just like the Beatles trying to do The Rolling Stones. The Rolling Stones can do it better".

Nevertheless, the soundtrack album, despite being dubbed "an utter travesty", defied the trend and was a hit, claiming a No. 5 spot in the US for five weeks and earning million-selling platinum status. 'Got to Get You into My Life' from Earth, Wind & Fire became a million-selling single, whilst 'Oh Darlin' ' from Robin, and 'Come Together' from Aerosmith, emerged unscathed from the brush with doom, hitting the top 40.

Still, RSO had to destroy hundreds of thousands of unsold copies, and the project inflicted a considerable financial loss upon Stigwood's company.

The Bee Gees smiled their way through the promotional interviews, but the film became a taboo subject and they studiously avoided mentioning it if at all possible, preferring, instead, to steer conversations towards their new album projects. Once again they found themselves pejoratively described as Beatles' imitators, and the anti-disco tsunami that suddenly loomed up took them along with it.

With hindsight, the Bee Gees would lay the blame for their declining popularity at the door of the film set. Partly true, for the set became inextricably linked with another growing problem for the Bee Gees; the struggle with drug addiction. Robin – who was "an odd person anyway, but when he was on pills, which he was for most of the time I knew him during his first marriage, he could say or do anything" according to former manager Chris Hutchins – would pump himself full of barbiturates so that he could go to sleep, and Mo was stunned by the sight of crew members bearing bags bulging with cocaine. All a long way from the days that Mo remembered when "we loved grass because it helped us create. But we were virginal compared to some others. I remember sitting in a room talking to John Lennon and I didn't realise he was tripping on acid".

Fans hadn't deserted them yet, though, and the unfortunately named Spirits Having Flown tour in 1979 through North America to support the album of the same name was a huge success.

The album had been released in January 1979 and produced by Barry, Albhy Galuten and Karl Richardson, who had worked long into the night creating it. Mo was battling alcohol, and his bass parts were given to a session musician, whilst both he and Robin were reduced to the roles of backing and harmony vocalists. In the end, Barry recorded most of those himself, too.

Nothing seemed to have changed when the single "Love You Inside Out" nestled on the No. 1 spot in the US and Canada in 1979, following on from the 1978 No. 1 spots for 'Too Much Heaven' and 'Tragedy' – also from the album, which itself hit the No. 1 spot in six major territories including the US and the UK. So business as usual? 14,000 fans packing the Fort Worth venue for the tour's opening night seemed to say so. And the boys wanted to reconnect with the people who supported them, get out of the stuffy studio environment and feel the love. And the love came to them, from a packed Madison Square Garden over three nights, for example, during which they rarely slept; Barry feigning ignorance over just how they managed to do that, citing their youth as the reason.

1979 was a year of superlatives; in January they received a star in the Hollywood Walk Of Fame. Four Grammy awards came their way in February and by mid-year, once 'Love You Inside Out' had hit the top spot, they had equalled the Beatles' record of charting six consecutive number one hits. Spirits Having Flown was about to become the most sought-after summer tour since the Fab Four.

Having missed the Billboard Awards – which accorded them 11 awards – because of rehearsals for the tour, the lads flew on a private jet (leased for $1,000,000 and bearing the Bee Gees' logo) to the venues to where five semi-trailers had transported a computer-guided set and its 40,000 light show computations. No hotels needed; the boys flew home to Miami after the gigs that brought in 800,000 fans to see them and earned some $10,000,000 in revenues, not to mention the merchandising raking in $3,000.00 – every minute. The statistics were phenomenal.

MAIN IMAGE:
The Bee Gees live in 1979 in San Francisco

For 38 venues and 41 dates, their largest tour ever, the boys brought the Bee Gees groove to the masses with audience attendances often well over 30,000 and venues never less than 90% full. In the L.A. Dodgers' stadium, filled with 60,000 fans, a plethora of celebrities from Barbara Streisand to Rod Stewart, Cary Grant to Jack Nicholson, Al Pacino to Olivia Newton-John, attended the show. Resplendent in their skin-tight, white satin pants and spangled white shirts with the familiar split to the midriff, the boys were often joined by Andy for 'You Should Be Dancing", to the deafening delight of the female fans and completing the illusion that all the Brothers Gibb were enclosed within the bosom of the group. Nothing to rock the Bee Gees' world. Disco might have been on life support, but the Bee Gees were the must-see band that year and giving the genre a final transfusion of glamour, replete with mirrored disco balls and glaring lighting. There was something for every fan; Barry's falsetto in 'Nights on Broadway' was the no-holds-barred production number, and the spotlight was also on Barry for 'Words', Robin recalled past times with 'How Can You Mend a Broken Heart', taking in 'Massachusetts' and 'I started a Joke' along the way, before the finale exploded with brass and lights and 'Jive Talkin' '. The encore, no doubt of there being one with the audience out of their seats and jiving in the isles, was 'You Should Be Dancing', and on the memorable night of the 30th of June in Houston, they were joined for the encore by John Travolta, shaking his hips à la Saturday Night Fever, who was taking a short break from filming Urban Cowboy.

Amongst the highlights came an honour that would certainly have pleased them enormously, for their efforts on behalf of UNICEF. Just before the concert on the 24th of September in Landover, Maryland, the Bee Gees were invited to the White House in Washington to be congratulated by President Carter for what they had done for the charity. They had appeared on an NBC TV show in aid of the charity in January that year and sung 'Too Much Heaven' for the United Nations General Assembly, and the revenues from their performance put around $7 million into UNICEF's funds.

There was even a country hit, 'Rest Your Love on Me', the B side of 'Too Much Heaven', which found its way into the top 40 on the country charts.

The tour had been accompanied by a team from NBC TV, making a 90-minute special for the network with British TV presenter David Frost, to be screened when the tour was over. It aired in November, and the boys were seen planning for the tour, relaxing in the wealthy area of Miami in Barry's house, in jamming sessions with Willie Nelson or Glen Campbell, and there was an interview with their parents, Hugh and Barbara, as well as with Robert Stigwood, and the lads were seen at work on their songs with Galuten, recording 'Tragedy'. There were thoughts about their facility for songwriting; "It's almost as though someone has already written the songs in the air and they're giving them to us", Barry mused. Mo added, "Most of the lyrics are written during the laying down of the back track" and once they got "that feeling" into the studio then "the fun really begins", Barry concluded the conversation. All this interspersed with plenty of footage of the concert performances, including from Andy.

So business as usual then in Bee Gees land.

Absolutely not, for Spirits Having Flown reflected the reality, and the Bee Gees found themselves in an unstoppable spiral downwards that only got worse as time passed. Disco had passed its sell-by date, and even as the Spirits tour got underway, the undertakers were donning

their top hats. To quote NPR, reporting on an American football game between the Chicago White Socks and the Detroit Tigers that year, "...a giant crate full of records was placed in the outfield. Dahl, the disgruntled disc jockey (24-year old Steve Dahl had been fired from a Chicago radio station that started playing disco only, and was then hired by a rival rock station – he got his revenge by destroying disco records on air), donned a combat helmet and military jacket and led chants of "disco sucks." Then they blew up the crate. The explosion scattered records high into the air and left a crater in centre field". Dahl subsequently wrote a book; Disco Demolition: The Night Disco Died.

It wasn't only Dahl who was on the warpath. The rock genre was forcing itself back out from beneath the platform shoes of the glamour boys, ready to take on the 80s. The charts were filled for the last time with Bee Gees' songs, for the new kids on the block would be wearing skinny black jeans and ties and using electronic synths. Discos were wiped out, too; the craze had passed, and the Bee Gees were being washed out of the door along with flares and tight pants. It had been an incredible half-decade, but the

MAIN IMAGE:
A Gift of Song concert at the United Nations General Assembly on January 9th 1979, New York

future was shadowy now. They'd resurrected themselves once, could they do it again? Did they even want to?

The demise was swift. There would never be another No. 1 album, and the next and final No. 1 single would be in 1987. The world was telling them that they had tired of Bee Gees' saturation. The lads needed to go and take stock of what the future held, and especially, for Mo, Robin and Andy to get their wayward characters back under control and instil a more manageable sense of order into their personal lives.

A two-year hiatus would arise before the next Bee Gees album appeared in the stores.

Mo recalled that period with mixed emotions. "It was just an amazing, crazy, extraordinary time. I remember not being able to answer the phone, and I remember people climbing over my walls. I was quite grateful when it stopped. It was too unreal. In the long run, your life is better if it's not like that on a constant basis. Nice though it was."

1980 would prove to be a fractured year of personal hills and valleys and a year when Barry's songwriting for others would take centre ground, whilst the Brothers Gibb took time out and thought about what it all meant. And fell victim to their own conservative approach to music.

First off was a project that Andy had been working on since the previous year, an album called After Dark. It was his last studio album and included duets with Olivia Newton-John; every song was written or co-written by Barry, who also added guitar and background and harmony vocals. A massive show of support from Barry. This album was the springboard for Barry's very successful writing and producing career during the next decade; he had assembled his team and was ready to go. Poor Andy was too gripped by drugs to be able to even sing. Mo had already spoken to his brother in no uncertain terms, telling him that all he had gained, house, money, friends and career, was in jeopardy if he didn't rein in his addictions.

MAIN IMAGE:
A 'live' portrait session in the photographer's studio on June 5, 1979 in Los Angeles

Andy probably understood, but it changed nothing. This led to a "heartbroken" Stigwood, who was finally forced to regard Andy as "the enemy", an enemy whose records didn't sell and who had become a highly problematic individual; Stigwood dropped him from his roster of stars, but only after he had tried to protect Andy from himself by staunching the money flow to drug barons. To no avail. Andy was the first of the Gibbs to fall off the branch.

The album, released in February 1980, reached only a disappointing No. 21 in the US, although the reviewers had been remarkably lenient, with later reviews recalling "a number of fine moments" such as 'Desire' and 'I Can't Help It', though neither fared well as a singles. Andy's dying career staggered on through the American TV show circuit that year. No one knew anything was wrong with the teenagers' favourite idol. He was even hired as co-host, alongside Dionne Warwick, of a TV show in September, Solid Gold, in which he had appeared as a singer several times and in which dancers would spin to the latest hit records.

Mo hadn't acted on his own advice to his brother and was also being slaughtered, by his drink problem. If action wasn't taken he would be going the way of Andy, and as there were thoughts of a new Bee Gees album, a healthy Mo was vital. Everyone in the family rallied around, including his wife, Yvonne. By mid year, she presented him with a choice; either go into rehab or their relationship would be over. Their new baby, Samantha, born in July, would also be gone with her. Mo saw the light and entered rehab in Santa Barbara, his first, but sadly not his last stay, this one accompanied by a back operation.

Robin, too, was only just keeping his head above water, but Molly wanted no more of it and filed for divorce in May of 1980. This pushed them into a battle of titanic horror. Robin, it seems, "desperately addicted to amphetamines", according to one newspaper report, hardly ate or slept, stayed up into the small hours writing songs, kept awake by speed until he swallowed the strong downers that would put him to sleep. According to the FBI files released in 2012, his confused brain told him that Molly, from whom he was now estranged, was plotting to fleece him of £5

million. So, together with a private detective he had hired who also acted as the getaway driver, he broke into her home in Weybridge in England looking for evidence. Technically, it was still his home, so she couldn't have him arrested; the documents he later presented to the British police and the FBI proved nothing at all. His paranoia reached such a state that, as FBI files revealed, he made death threats to Molly's London lawyers on one occasion. One telegram to her solicitors, Haymon and Walters, stated that he had hired a hitman; "The situation is now very serious... no one walks all over me... I have had enough. I have taken out a contract. It is now a question of time".

As the court battle dragged on, Robin was forbidden to see his children, Spencer and Melissa, a state that would continue for the next six years and drive Robin to "the verge of madness", as he confessed later. He'd even been arrested and given a 14-day (suspended) sentence for talking to the press about the marriage in contravention of a court order. A tragic fall from grace for a man who had had the world at his feet, but couldn't silence his personal demons. "You can achieve great things in life professionally, but if your children are being kept away from you, you feel empty. I had some of my blackest moments during those lost years", Robin recalled later.

Molly showed herself more compassionate once he had called off his dogs, reluctantly, and allowed the children to see him.

By then, Robin had met his second wife Dwina Murphy. Dwina was a druid priestess, and her sexually open lifestyle suited Robin. Through her influence, he broke his drink and drug habits and became a vegan, but still indulged his ravenous sexual appetites. But the couple had a son in 1983, Robin John, and were married for 27 years until death parted them.

Barry showed what could be achieved by avoiding the twin perils of excessive drink and drug consumption; he not only bought a new mansion in Miami to add to his 36-acre estate outside London, UK, eventually accumulating property worth $20 million, he also undertook to write and sing with Barbara Streisand.

Streisand's career had also dipped, and by 1979 she was looking for a way to revitalise it. She had seized upon Barry as the ideal producer, composer for her when she turned up at the boys' concert at the Dodgers' stadium. Barry had heard of her reputation for being difficult, but Neil Diamond assured him in a phone call that she was fantastic to work with and that he should not hesitate. Barry, glad to try to steer himself onto a different track, enlisted Robin and Galuten's help and off they went.

A consummate professional, Barry knew Streisand's strengths and weaknesses and wanted to bring something new to her repertoire and the singer back into the mainstream. He brought his writing talents to bear on all of the nine tracks, with Robin working on five. The album would be called Guilty.

Released in September 1980, Guilty catapulted the star back into the spotlight with her best-selling album ever and several hit singles of which 'Woman in Love' went to the top and was her biggest hit of the decade, spending three weeks on the UK No. 1. spot. Her vocals were astonishing, sensuous and powerful, and the album became a 15-million sales hit. 'Woman in Love' was a collaboration between Barry and Robin and they picked up the British Ivor Novello Award for best song musically and lyrically. Streisand received a Grammy for Best Pop Vocal Performance by a Duo or Group. For Barry, success continued to smile on him without the stress of being one of the Bee Gees', though he later confessed to being somewhat peeved that his role in the Streisand success story had not been generally perceived to be as great as it was, but without pointing any fingers towards a particular culprit; no fault of Streisand's. The reason that the Streisand album was not a fully-fledged Bee Gees' package was that Mo was teetering on the edge of implosion from his drinking problems.

Andy finally had a positive experience in his personal life that year. During his Solid Gold show period, he also appeared in a TV show with host John Davidson and was

LEFT:
Bee Gees portrait on August 8, 1979

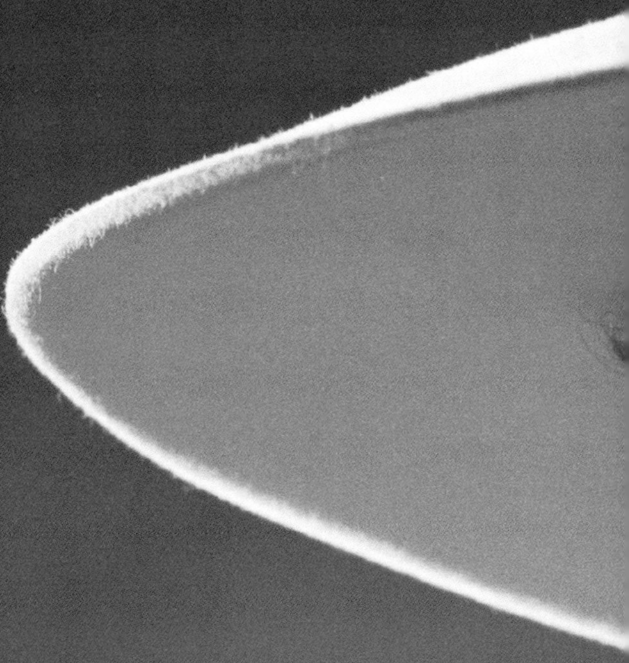

brought face to face with Victoria Principal, star of Dallas. She was already enamoured of the young singer, and when he met her, it was plain that he had fallen heavily for her, too. In the blink of an eye, they were a couple and the toast of Hollywood. They kissed in public, they smiled for photographs and began to talk of getting married. And what more natural progression then, but to sing together, à la Barry and Streisand. As befitted star-crossed lovers, they chose 'All I have to do is Dream' by the Everly Brothers. They would sing it on Andy's Solid Gold show on TV. So he and the "not only a beautiful and talented actress, but a special friend", as Robin introduced her, indulged in some mushy lovers' talk before they duetted for each other.

It all seemed too good to be true, although, for a while, it was true and good. But without getting his private menagerie of neuroses in check, as Mo had done, there was little hope for any of his relationships. Newspapers reported his consumption of one thousand dollars' worth of coke a day. He was hired to work on the production of Pirates of Penzance, but his gentle voice couldn't carry in a large theatre, and before long he was sacked. His ego took another battering, and Victoria saw the writing on the wall, presenting him with a familiar ultimatum in Gibb life; drugs or her. He chose drugs, and another public implosion of a Bee Gee took place. His self-pity was plastered all over the dailies; "I wanted to commit suicide".

In later years, Andy is quoted as saying, somewhat disingenuously, that the breakup with Victoria made him turn to drugs for consolation, that he loved Victoria and always would, she was the most generous person. He wondered if "I'll ever have the courage to give myself so completely to another human being... when we split, I just fell apart". Newspapers reported that he had given himself over to drugs for an entire month after the breakup.

But soon, In TV shows, Robin was insisting that the drug habit was behind him, although he began to exhibit more self-pity, expressing incomprehension that Victoria "didn't seem to go through any pain", and had closed down on him emotionally. "It really was hell for me. I had a nervous breakdown." Victoria, on the other hand, recorded that their breakup was "preceded and precipitated by drugs. She had, she said, done "everything I could to help him". There was not one more thing she could do to save Andy, she added. "I knew I had to leave in order to save myself". Addiction had been victorious once again.

Drugs still had a hold on Andy it would seem. He was still delivering pink cotton-wool dialogue on his Solid Gold TV show with his co-star singer Marilyn McCoo, duetting with his guests such as Marie Osmond. But the drugs were permeating into his professional life, and rumours abounded that two versions of the show would be prepared each week, one with Andy, and the other as a fail-safe for when he was unable to show up yet again. Probably downed by his addictions once more. As a result, he was dropped from the show after just one season.

MAIN IMAGE:
Andy Gibb in London in February 1980

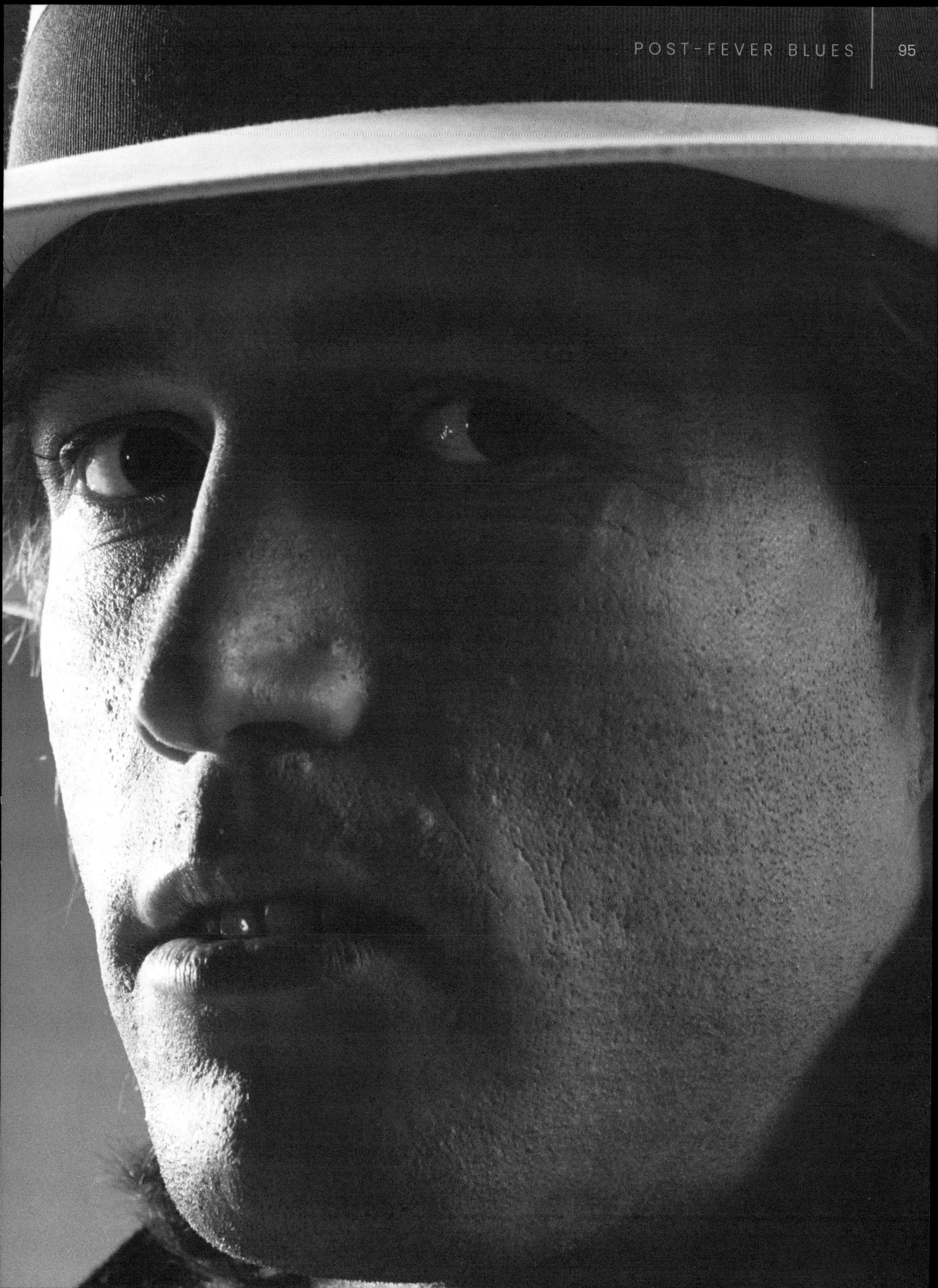

EIGHTIES MEMORABILIA

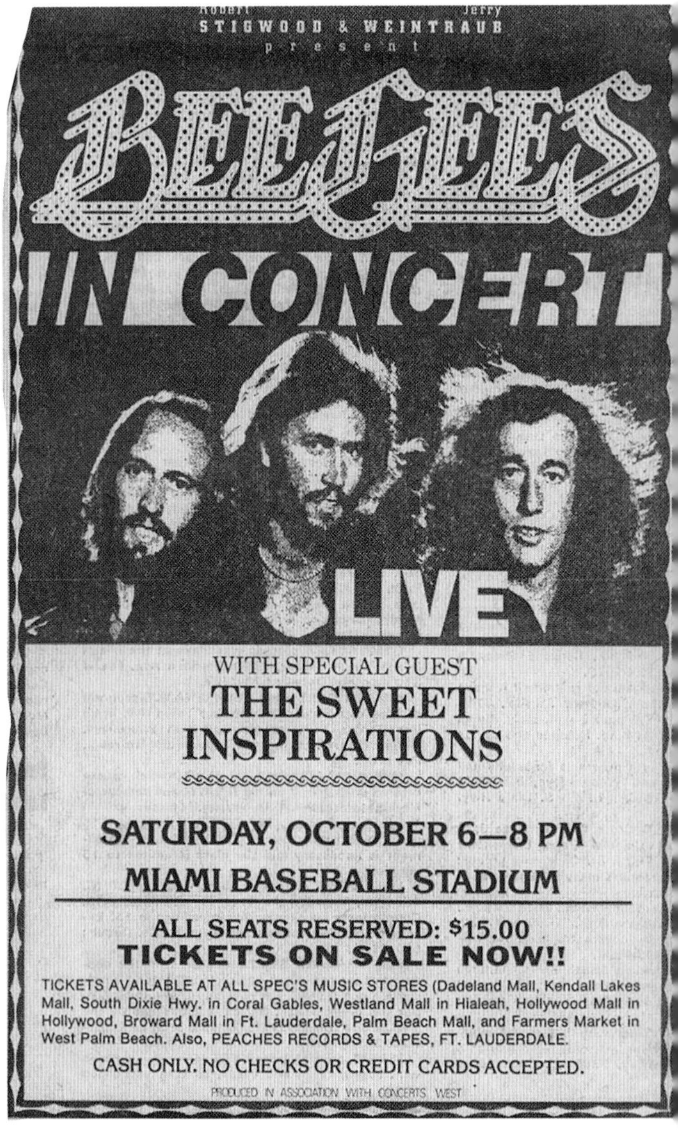

PRESS RELEASE

WARNER BROS. RECORDS, INC. / 3300 WARNER BOULEVARD / BURBANK, CALIFORNIA 91510 (818) 953-3223

BEE GEES ANNOUNCE 1989 "ONE FOR ALL"

EUROPEAN TOUR DATES

The Bee Gees, currently in intensive rehearsals in England, are set to embark on their first European tour in over 15 years commencing May 3rd in Dortmund, Germany and including 35 dates in 24 cities, including 3 performances at London's Wembley Arena. Ticket sales for the Bee Gees 1989 One For All tour, coinciding with the release in Europe of their new Warner Bros. Records album One have already topped the quarter-million mark with venues already sold out in most cities. The group is additionally exploring the possibility of a North American tour later this year.

One, the Bee Gees 26th LP in 25 years, has just been released on the continent and has yielded the group's latest single, "Ordinary Lives." The album is scheduled for release stateside in August. Various cuts from the album will be featured in the legendary group's concert set, which will also include such Bee Gee perennials as "Jive Talkin'," "Nights On Broadway," "Massachusetts," "Stayin' Alive," "Lonely Days," "Words," "How Deep Is Your Love" and One selections "House of Shame," "Wish You Were Here," "It's My Neighborhood," the above-mentioned "Ordinary Lives" and the album's title track.

Joining the Bee Gees on stage will be guitarists Tim Cansfield and Alan Kendall, keyboardists Gary Moberley and Vic Martin, drummer Chester Thompson, bassist George Perry and back-up singers Linda Harmon, Tampa Lann and Phyllis St. James.

75 ROCKEFELLER PLAZA / 20th FLOOR / NEW YORK, NEW YORK 10019 / (212) 484-6800
1815 DIVISION STREET / POST OFFICE BOX 120897 / NASHVILLE, TENNESSEE 37212 / (615) 320-7525

BEE GEES
ONE FOR ALL TOUR
LIVE IN AUSTRALIA 1989

one
BEE GEES
tour
for all
89

DESCENT INTO TRAGEDY

October 1981 saw the release of their 16th original album, Living Eyes. Not a success, although it struggled into the top 40 of several territories; radio stations were no longer playing Bee Gees' songs, so strongly were their reputations tied to the defunct disco genre.

Barry realised too late the mistake they had made, although he felt that it was "our finest album in terms of depth, performance and quality of the production". Having spent some 11 months working on the album, it must have been hard for Barry to admit that, "Obviously, we had a scare with Living Eyes. It wasn't the kind of album we should have brought out at that point. It was a little too downbeat, as opposed to having energy".

Aware that they needed to change direction, they sought to do so, moving away from falsetto vocals, trying something different. It didn't work. In fact, it was "a turkey", as Robin put it. Which was not how it was regarded in later years when the words "a real gem" were applied to it; "a decent and highly listenable album". In fact, one reviewer could only find fault with the track 'He's a Liar', which he thought contained weak vocals and thematically led up a dead end.

Whether the problem was over-exposure, the Sgt. Pepper debacle hanging over them still, or the scent of disco that persisted in clinging to them, the album and its singles did not fare well. The Bee Gees, with their hairy chests exposed and high voices, now supplied material for a string of comedy sketches. Barry was at a loss to comprehend the swift change in public taste; "It was almost like people were angry with us and it was more interesting to make fun of us than to actually try and understand or appreciate what we had done" he mused, whereas Robin astutely remarked, "The public had od'd on us." The Bee Gees would not release another album until 1987.

Maurice was the hardest hit by this downturn, and he increased his drink and drug consumption. That year of 1981, his drunk and disorderly behaviour saw him thrown off the Concorde. Rumours spread that a breakup was imminent. The boys were exhausted and the way forward was shrouded in uncertainty. Barry kept them together and working, composing hits for other artists. (One of the greatest was for Dionne Warwick in 1982, 'Heartbreaker', which she took to the top of the charts. The Gibb brothers composed 6 of the songs, Barry, who was also co-producer, and Galuten the other 3. The success of the album proved that they truly were hit-smiths, yet it sent Maurice into an agony of self-pity; Mo confessed later that, "I cried my eyes out after we wrote it. I drove home and thought, 'We should be doing this one'". There had been no chart-breakers for the lads since 1979, after all.)

The album Heartbreaker was released in September 1982 and reached No. 3 in the UK and the Top 30 in the US.

Andy was now in deep trouble. Yet, despite his problems, he was hired again for another musical, this time Joseph and the Amazing Technicolour Dreamcoat on Broadway, a project that filled him with delight. Just not enough delight to prevent a repeat of his problems. Although he loved being in the show and being one of the actors, despite his financial generosity and the good will of all around him, he started to miss performances on the pre-New York run, and then didn't appear for dress rehearsals in New York and failed to turn up for a series of performances after the show opened. His fellow actors thought that he was plagued by stage fright, which was more likely to have scuppered his chances than

RIGHT:

Bee Gees portrait, Italy, 1986

the consumption of drugs, although it's unlikely he'd been able to keep that in check during such a stressful time. Most of the time, his fellow actors reported, Andy was slumped into a chair staring at the TV. It did not bode well.

Eight performances a week were more than Andy, now 24 years old, had been able to cope with. It was an untenable situation for the producers and the many disappointed audiences. Producer Zev Bufman finally took him aside and told him that the end had been reached and he had to turn up for every performance. Andy was willing and offered to leave the show if he missed another show.

> With six weeks on Broadway under its belt, Joseph lost its star when he was fired, having had one of his blowouts.

It was the beginning of the end for the wayward Gibb; he'd lost his TV show, his record label, his management, his girlfriend.

One optimistic agent persuaded him to work on a Las Vegas style show, which he could take out on the road. Andy did and was praised for his performance; audiences were enthusiastic. Success, it seemed, was his again for the taking; yet in his depressed mental state, all he could see was failure.

Robin began work on his first solo album since 1970 and enlisted Mo's support. How Old Are You? failed to make any impact on the major charts upon its release in 1983 with its new wave, pop-rock, soft-rock and synth-pop styles.

Barry, buoyed by his songwriter/production successes, now took on Kenny Rogers, who, like Streisand and Dionne Warwick, was looking to revive his career. He had to agree to recording an entire album before Barry would take him on. He did, but when the song 'Islands in the Stream' failed to glitter in the studio, Dolly Parton was brought on board. Parton was now showbiz royalty, and with her voice, the song shot up the charts to hit the number one spot in October 1983 selling millions of copies, making it one of the most successful country-pop hits ever.

The album itself, Eyes That See in the Dark, was also hugely successful with the Brothers Gibb involved in creating each of the ten tracks. It went to No. 1 in the US and No. 5 in Canada.

By 1983, Andy was drowning both personally and professionally. He was still suffering from being the younger Gibb, unable to escape questions about the Bee Gees wherever he went. He appeared on a TV show that could boast having hosted many high-calibre stars from Sammy Davis Junior to Whitney Houston, and in a sitcom called Gimme a Break. Andy was about to fall in love again, unbeknown to anyone, for the last time. He couldn't take his eyes off one of the stars of the show, Kari Michaelsen.

They were soon inseparable off the set and kept a low profile when out and about. But the romance was a beautiful, brief mirage that flared and died when Andy succumbed to drugs and paranoia, which meant that he would spend weeks without contacting her, unwilling to let her see him in the grip of his demons or share with her what he done or where he had been.

In February and March 1983, the Bee Gees gathered for another Robert Stigwood project. Buoyed by the success of Saturday Night Fever, Stigwood was making another dance movie, and asked the Bee Gees to compose new songs for the soundtrack for a sequel to Fever. Staying Alive would be the boys' final contractual obligation to RSO. And John Travolta was back on board as Tony, still down on his luck. Sylvester Stallone had been recruited as director.

The lads composed six songs, including a new recording of 'Stayin' Alive' as the film's theme song. However, the brothers' compositions, although as smooth and well-made as ever, lacked their Fever flair, and the singles 'The Woman in You' and 'Someone Belonging to Someone' went nowhere. Ironically, the only song that did become a hit was sung by Stallone's brother, Frank. Written by Frank and Vince DiCola, 'Far From Over' was a top-ten US single in September 1983, settling at No. 10 on the Billboard Hot 100.

Reviews for the film were lukewarm. It was just an attempt

MAIN IMAGE:
The Bee Gees perform in 1985

to leap on the bandwagon and not a ground-breaking look behind the curtain of contemporary life. Nonetheless, it, too, would be a box-office success though not achieving the status of Fever.

Thus the project seemed to reflect the Bee Gees' own trajectory, and interviewers, too, had taken the faded glory theme on board and presented the boys with the uncomfortable truth as they went around promoting the film and themselves.

Although promoting themselves on tours and albums seemed to have lost its enticements for the boys; instead, they would hunker down and compose songs for others

to enjoy the success, whilst they, Mo, Robin and Andy at least, tried to re-float the listing ships of their personal lives. There were also other niggling problems such as the law suit brought against them in 1983 for allegedly stealing material for 'How Deep is Your Love' from the song 'Let it End' by songwriter Ronald Selle. It was irritating but finally decided in the Gibbs' favour.

And for Barry, there was work enough. Later that year, he started on his solo project Now Voyager, which would also spawn a film, and signed a multi-million dollar deal with MCA, so that much of his time stretching into 1984 was spent writing and recording. 'Fine Line' and 'Shine Shine' did fairly well in the US charts with 'Shine Shine' climbing to No. 8 in the Hot 100 Adult Contemporary chart.

Robin also produced a solo album released in 1985, Walls Have Eyes, on which Barry co-wrote eight of the ten tracks. Walls fared badly, only scraping in at No. 27 in Canada.

And the next candidate for a musical resurrection was soon knocking at composer Barry's door. Diana Ross had shot to fame with The Supremes in the 1960s and 70s, but the years since her last success were beginning to add up.

In 1985, Barry and the others went to work immediately on songs for her album Eaten Alive, and Barry came up with 'Chain Reaction'. The trouble with it was that it was

MAIN IMAGE:

so Motown that it harked back to the golden age, and the boys feared that it would not be at all what she wanted.

They needn't have worried, for although she had slight misgivings, she understood the references to her success, and the song climbed high in the UK charts and was a hit in Australia, too. Eaten Alive hit No. 1 in the Uk, Australia and Ireland.

Having released another version of 'Hold Her in Your Hand' in 1984, in 1985, Mo composed and recorded the instrumental The Supernaturals, which served as a soundtrack for the film of the same name.

Andy, who had two successful gigs in 1984 and 1985 at the Riviera Hotel in Las Vegas, finally caved in and entered the Betty Ford Clinic in 1985. He needed comfort and asked Kari Michaelsen to visit him, which she willingly did, bringing a guitar and encouraging him to write. Gradually, he began to come back to life.

When he left the clinic, he was determined to get the next part of his life right, so he moved from his house in Malibu with its bad memories, and joined Alcoholics Anonymous. His willpower was weaker than his desire, sadly, and he dipped back into his vices, losing Kari a second time in the process. On TV he confessed to the world that he had had a nervous breakdown. He knew he had hurt many people and himself and expressed the wish to never go through it all again.

But Andy's life had nose-dived; he could barely command $2000 a month to live on now, and his reckless life style would soon lead to a declaration of bankruptcy.

As 1986 came to end, the Bee Gees had become estranged from Robert Stigwood, suing him for royalties to the tune of $75 million and the return of copyrights and masters. So they were searching for another label.

Also the muse had visited them again, desirous of another album. The years had flushed out the odour of disco, and it was time to get back into the fray. Their choice was Warner Bros., where Eric Clapton was now at home; it seemed a

propitious choice. E.S.P would be their 17th studio album, Arif Mardin was back on board, and they began work in September.

Over the years, the boys had acquired different recording styles; Barry would write songs, record demos and then polish these with session players in the studio. Morris liked to be involved in the production and work with session players during recording, whilst Robin also preferred to work his songs out during recording sessions. On E.S.P., each of them made their own recordings to be completed in the studio with the session players. Barry wrote five of the songs and was involved in all but two of the other 11. One reviewer would remark that, "Most of the songs sport contemporary, techno-style arrangements that rely heavily on synthesiser and drum machines", which, he said, showed that the brothers had kept their ear to the musical ground and knew what a new dawn required. And it was Barry who wrote the melody for what would become their first number one hit in many years, 'You Win Again'. Apparently, Barry had woken up in the middle of the night with the melody playing in his head; he always kept the tape recorder beside his bed. The band knew instinctively that it would be a hit and devoted an entire month to recording it. For their efforts, they were rewarded with a No. 1 single in Britain, Ireland, Switzerland, Germany, Austria, Denmark and Norway. The Bee Gees became the first group to have topped the charts in the 1960s, 70s and 80s, and the single brought them in another Ivor Novello award. It was quite some comeback.

Nonetheless, a change had taken place in the intervening years. The brothers might now call Miami their home, enjoying the warmth, and the relative proximity off New York, Britain and California, but the Americans had fallen out of love with the eternal smiles and tight pants; fortunately for the lads, Europe was now taking up the slack as their latest album proved, having hit the No. 5 spot in both the UK and the European Albums charts, and No. 1 in both Germany and Switzerland. Europe had "given us back the respect we had before Fever" Barry said. They intended to capitalise on that enthusiasm by going on a world tour.

MAIN IMAGE:

Only Andy was still causing consternation; Robin Gibb, saw his brother go "downhill so fast... he was in a terrible state of depression" after the breakup with Victoria Principal. He owed Stigwood $1 million and declared bankruptcy. His health had taken a battering, and while hospitalised he had been diagnosed with a heart infection, myocarditis, from cocaine abuse. If he were to continue taking cocaine, it could prove fatal.

When he was well enough, he worked on four new songs with Barry and relocated to Oxfordshire in England. He was hopeful that his life had changed finally for the better. "Mum's going to look after me and play mum. I'm going to concentrate on music and I expect to have an album out this spring" he announced.

Andy loved flying. He was taking lessons and found that, as he put it, there was no better way to leave problems behind. "We only go around once, so why not enjoy it? I'm going to live life to the fullest."

"I just adore that boy, he has the kindest nature imaginable" his mother said about him, and, whilst musing that he'd always been a risk-taker, she admitted that she would prefer to have him "beside me with his two feet planted firmly on the ground".

Andy stayed with Robin, living on the $200 a week that his brothers gave him. Which enabled him to take off secretly and buy himself alcohol. He began bingeing

phone call.

Their angry worry was justified, for shortly afterwards, Andy was delivered into hospital with chest pains.

At some time around 8:30 on the morning of the 10th of March 1988, Andy was informed by his doctor that to determine the cause of his chest pains, more tests would have to be carried out. But it was too late. Andy became unconsciousness later in the day and the myocarditis finally killed him. A glittering career had smashed tragically into the ground.

The others were plagued by guilt, questioning if they had done all they could to help him. Andy's death was, said Barry, "The saddest moment of my life", and reproached himself for ever having started his sibling on his music career, a career that had taken him to incredible success, incredible heartache. Andy had succumbed, as so many had before him, to the allure of a life that was a drug-induced mirage.

Everyone was grief-stricken at the waste of such a young life, but none more so than Barbara, his mother. Such was the shock to her, that there were reports that she had required sedation after his death.

Andy was laid to rest in Forest Lawn in Los Angeles.

MAIN IMAGE:
Andy Gibb in the 1980s

THE PAST CLAIMS ITS OWN

The Bee Gees could only keep moving forwards. They'd been working on their album One when Andy died, and they only started recording again in November of 1988, moving the project to the Mayfair Studios in London

The album was released the following year, a melancholic offering, unsurprisingly, which contained a tribute to the brother they had lost; 'Wish You Were Here'. That single reached No. 7 in the US, but the album was not generally successful, although Rolling Stone later called it underrated. "It ain't no party, it ain't no disco, it ain't no fooling around" wrote the reviewer. The band would be happy with that.

Nonetheless, the brothers had decided to go out on tour after a ten-year hiatus, and set off on the One for All tour, starting in Germany on May 3rd 1989 and visiting 19 cities; in Europe they could still pull the crowds. There was little talk there of the Bee Gees as a has-been disco band, an accusation that irked the normally cautious Barry into sarcasm in interviews when the subject of disco raised it maligned head. Now the boys dressed in the style each preferred; tailored suits for Robin, leather jackets for Mo, blue jeans and shirts.

So, even though back problems were making life difficult for Barry to the extent that he even considered having surgery, they presented the fans with 30 years of Bee Gees' favourites and songs they'd written for other singers, harmonising superbly, and concluded the tour in Australia to sold-out venues; modern, schmalzy, a love fest, everyone loved the show and went home happy.

Searching for a new sound direction again, in 1991 the Bee Gees released the album High Civilisation. With drum programming prominent and electronic effects included, there was more modern dance groove to the recordings. The fans weren't enthusiastic, except in German-speaking countries, and the album wasn't a great success, charting at No. 24 in the UK. A short tour followed.

Barry 's back problem became so serious that it required surgery. And he was now being plagued by arthritis in his back, right hand and right knee, which became so severe that he feared he would soon be forced to stop playing the guitar.

Mo was still a slave to alcohol, claiming to have downed four bottles of whiskey, two of brandy and gallons of Guinness when Yvonne and the children were away for a while. Mo's personal demon took on a more sinister shape. Brandy was consumed neat, and the low point came in 1991, when Maurice threatened his family with a gun. Yvonne took the kids and escaped from the house.

Part of his problem stemmed from a sense of being frustrated, like Andy. Chris Hutchins, former Bee Gees press agent, said in a radio interview that Maurice had "greatly weakened" himself through his drinking and was a "tormented soul", longing to be the group's lead singer.

RIGHT:

BG2K Millennium Concert at the National Car Rental Center, December 31, 1999, Sunrise, Florida

After Barry told Maurice that there was no more support for him in the family, Mo finally recognised the danger and got himself into rehab before anything worse happened. With the help of others on the 28-day program, he came to understand what had happened to him and why; how fame had consumed him, how he was also consumed by self-loathing, doubt and insecurity, just as Andy had been. Stripped of the trappings of wealth, he slowly returned to earth.

Maurice even went public in an interview with Lynn Redgrave in 1992, perhaps hoping that a public confession would help to shame him into abstention. He spoke about the performances when he was blind drunk, when session players would have to fill in his bass parts. There was a confession that, as his intoxication worsened, his mornings were spent vomiting, before the first drink; his liver was in trouble, his behaviour was abusive, belligerent and arrogant.

Mo persisted through another program and worked hard to win back his family; fortunately he managed to do it, and he and Yvonne eventually retook their wedding vows. For Mo, life was starting again.

But for Hugh Gibb, life had run its course; he died of internal bleeding the same year. Unsurprisingly, Barry believed that Andy's demise had played its part in his death, that Hugh had simply given up.

Still hunting the elusive sound that would break the Gordian Knot tying them to a chart life outside the USA, the brothers produced Size isn't Everything in 1993. They abandoned the dance sound, seeking solace in a pre-Saturday Night Fever Bee Gees' world. But the US remained uninterested in the Bee Gees. It was left to the British to salvage their pride, which they did upon the release of 'Paying the Price of Love', the first single release on the 9th of August 1993. It came in at No. 23. In late September, the album reached No. 33 before slipping from the charts only to reappear in December following the release of 'For Whom the Bell Tolls', the second single. When that single arrived in the top ten, the album went up to No. 23. With the third single, 'How to Fall in Love Part 1' settling at No. 30, a Bee Gees album contained three UK top 30s for the first time since 1979.

> And there they left album recording for another few years.

The intervening time was spent writing songs for other artists and for a potential new album, which would not appear until 1997, performances such as the one given for the Royal Variety Performance before the British Queen at the London Dominion Theatre, or being involved with a biographical documentary about themselves. Maurice kept busy producing recordings for his daughter Samantha.

> As 1997 came around, they were ready for another bite at the cherry.

The year got off to a good start with an International Artist Award in L.A. on January the 27th, an enthusiastic audience dancing to the Bee Gees again, just as they had many years before. It was a wonderful confirmation of the boys' huge contribution to music.

Still Waters was ready to go and hit the streets in March. It brought together songs that had been written at various times over the last few years. It didn't fare well at the hands of the critics, but the buying public thought differently and lifted it to No. 2 in the UK and, gratifyingly, No. 11 in the US.

MAIN IMAGE:
Live at Ahoy in Rotterdam, Netherland, 1998

The UK bought the single, too, 'Alone', which got to No. 5 and even reached No. 1 in Canada.

Barry was still in pain with his back and unwilling to tour at 51. But after the success of a CD from a show performed at Las Vegas, Barry reluctantly allowed himself to be talked into further one-night gigs that eventually took them all around the world. Gone was the soured disco-era aura; the boys now sported long leather coats. Andy was remembered and celebrated, and if Barry's falsetto was not what it used to be, the 72,000 Australians in the audience in Sydney in 1999 cared not; the Bee Gees were pop gods and the beat and the dancing went on.

For one night only.

For the Brothers Gibb would never play to their Australian audiences again.

The years were passing and five decades of recording was celebrated by another album – although no one could know in 2001 that it was to be the last that the Bee Gees would produce; This Is Where I Came In. Maurice, who had been through so much pain, bravely sang 'Man in the Middle', the place he had now come to accept as his in the group, the peacemaker, the smoother of egos.

With the title song 'This is Where I came In' finding a place at No. 18 in the UK, 23 in the US, the album itself did well, finding the No. 6 spot in the UK and even No. 16 in the US. But this time there were to be no tours. Time had taken its toll. Time demanded a period of rest for the brothers; they wanted time to reflect.

But not to be inactive.

In 2002, came the announcement of the Queen's New Year's Honours List; Barry, Robin and Maurice were to be awarded CBE's (Commander Of The British Empire) in recognition of their services to music.

They played at the Love and Hope Ball, which turned out to be another farewell; it was the last concert the Bee Gees would play as a trio.

Barry started to work with his friend Michael Jackson, and Maurice was keeping his life low-key, playing paintball, whilst Robin worked on his latest album, Magnet.

But then they arrived in 2003.

The bad news followed quickly.

Maurice had been rushed to hospital. It was the 12th of January. He was suffering from stomach pain; an intestinal blockage was diagnosed and the doctors operated.

With his wife and children at his bedside, Maurice suffered a heart attack and died on the night of the 11th to the 12th of January.

Mo, always so ready to have fun, who had struggled and finally beaten the demons that had made his personal life hell; it was so unfair. Everyone was devastated.

"It's like a nightmare... I can't accept that he's dead. I just imagine he's alive somewhere else" said Robin, struggling to cope with his brother's demise.

MAIN IMAGE:

Live at Ahoy in Rotterdam, Netherlands, 1998

Barry was tortured by the memory that he and Maurice had been at odds at the time of Mo's death. Now he would have to live with the thought that after a lifetime of closeness, they had never reconciled. The Bee Gees would continue to play, he insisted, for themselves and to keep alive the memory of their brother.

Robin, however, had come to his own conclusions, saying that the Bee Gees had been three brothers; "It's Maurice's name; we would respect that and not to be the Bee Gees any more... we don't want to be the Bee Gees again."

It was over. The lights had gone out. The remaining two Bee Gees had reverted to being the Gibb brothers.

But brothers who were slowly moving apart. Mo had been the invisible glue that had held them together. Without him, Robin and Barry were no longer even friends, according to Barry; their business interests moved in different directions and they didn't speak to one another for over a year.

By 2003, Barry was telling the world that he and Robin had been reconciled, but the distance between their houses, with Robin in England and Barry in Florida, seemed symbolic for what had once been a family relationship impenetrable to outsiders.

Robin went on with his solo performances, and the brothers finally got together again for the One World Project in 2005 to raise money for relief for the Indian ocean earthquake and tsunami. They also performed together in 2006 for two concerts, one in Miami, and the other for the Princes Trust 30th Birthday Concert at the Tower of London.

But Robin was not well even then; looking drawn and stick-insect thin, in 2010 he had surgery in Oxford in England for a blocked intestine, and cancelled performances. One year later, in November 2011, Robin was 61 years old, the diagnosis was colorectal cancer that had spread to his liver.

Robin was dying.

Barry visited him in hospital and kissed his brother's forehead.

Robin underwent chemotherapy, but by March 2012, he was forced to undergo another operation. The cancer had reached an advanced stage; pneumonia set in, and Robin fell into a coma. Once, briefly, he regained consciousness; but on May the 20th, he died.

Now alone, regretting that he had also become alienated from Robin, as he had been from Mo, Barry was grief-stricken at the loss of the last of his brothers.

Remembered by so many as a friend to all who knew him, talented and generous, when Robin died, an incredible music journey that had taken four young lads from the Isle of Man to musical.superstardom, and then taken three of them from the world in return, had come to an end.

RIGHT:
KIIS-FM's 'Wango Tango' two day concert series at Dodger Stadium in Los Angeles, 2001

BARRY GIBB

Sir Barry Alan Crompton Gibb, CBE, was born on the Isle of Man, United Kingdom on the 1st of September 1946. He was the second child of bandleader Hugh Gibb and his wife Barbara and started attending Braddan school shortly after his fifth birthday on the 4th of September 1951.

Barry formed a skiffle group with his younger brothers Maurice and Robin, called The Rattlesnakes, in 1955, and their first professional gig was at the Gaumont Cinema on the 28th of December 1957.

When the family moved to Australia in 1958, their talents were spotted by a local DJ, and when Barry left school in 1961 and the family moved to Surfers Paradise, the brothers would perform in clubs and hotels during the summer. They now called themselves the Bee Gees and Barry sang and played guitar.

At the beginning of 1963, the family moved again, to Sydney. They signed a deal with Festival Records, and Barry composed all of the songs for the group between 1963 and 1966.

Barry's song, 'I Was a Lover, A Leader of Men', won him an annual Radio 5KA award for the best composition of the year.

In 1967, the Bee Gees were back in England, represented by Robert Stigwood. It was the start of a stellar career, but one which left Barry in a state of physical and mental exhaustion before the year was out. The pop-psychedelic single 'New York Mining Disaster 1941', which Barry co-wrote with Robin, became their first international success. Barry would often take the role of lead singer and became the de facto leader of the group.

In the 1970s, with the group reinventing themselves and playing dance-oriented music, Barry adopted a falsetto singing voice which became the band's trade mark for their successful careers during the disco era. Barry was adopted as a sex symbol by the fans and played the role to the full, with a gold chain, a long mane of hair and shirts open to the waist.

As a prolific songwriter, Barry worked with other artists, including Kenny Rogers, Barbra Streisand and Dionne Warwick.

Following the loss of his three brothers, Barry continued to record and perform despite health problems – he suffered from back problems and arthritis for many years. He debuted at Grand Ole Opry in 2012 and went on a world tour in 2013, touring the US in 2014. He also appeared at many festivals such as the Hard Rock Rising Miami Beach Global Music Festival alongside stars such as Andrea Bochelli. In 2016 he signed to Columbia Records for a new album.

Barry Gibb has written two solo albums, Now Voyager from 1984 and In the Now from 2016. He also wrote the soundtrack for Hawks in 1988.

Barry Gibb was formerly married to Maureen Bates from whom he was divorced in 1970. He married Linda Gray on the 1st of September 1970 and they have five children.

As a holder of dual citizenship, Barry Gibb divides his time between the US and the UK.

ROBIN GIBB

Robin Hugh Gibb, CBE, was born in the Jane Crookall Maternity Home in Douglas on the Isle of Man, United Kingdom on the 22nd of December 1949, just 30 minutes ahead of his twin brother, Maurice.

Their characteristic three-part harmonies could then be heard on their first single release in 1963, 'The Battle of the Blue and the Grey'. Robin and Barry shared the lead singer spot, and it was Robin and Barry who wrote most of the group's original songs.

Soon, they had renamed the band, The Bee Gees.

Having returned to England in 1967, before long The Bee Gees were tasting success with a Robin and Barry song, the psychedelic rock-oriented 'New York Mining Disaster, 1941'.

Robin collapsed with exhaustion in 1968, falling unconscious, and was admitted to a London nursing home; he later suffered relapses so that the first US tour had to be cancelled. Robin started taking drugs in his teens and later fell into a hedonistic lifestyle that ruined his health. This was the year that he married Molly Hullis, a secretary in Robert Stigwood's RSO organisation. They had two children, Spencer and Melissa. Molly would file for divorce on the 22nd of May 1980 after Robin's drug-induced paranoia became intolerable.

Robin remarried, to Dwina Murphy, a relationship that survived Robin's eight-year affair with his housekeeper and produced a daughter, Snow Evelyn Robin Juliet, and endured until his death.

Robin found himself at odds with Barry's dominance, and left the band to go it alone, with his solo album, 'Robin's Reign', released in 1970. His first hit was 'Saved by the Bell'. Robin and his brothers reunited later that year.

Despite the band's phenomenal disco-era successes, Robin continued to clash both personally and professionally with Barry and still consumed drugs. Nonetheless, he collaborated with his brothers to write hit songs for other artists such as Dionne Warwick.

When Maurice died in 2003, Robin announced that the Bee Gees would not re-form, and released his fifth solo album, Magnet, starting a second solo career.

In 2010, Robin's former drug abuse caught up with him and he was admitted to hospital with stomach pains. Over the following two years his health deteriorated, and he died in London on the 20th of May 2012 at the age of 62 from liver and kidney failure.

Robin had been inducted into the Songwriters Hall of Fame at the Grammy Museum in 1994, and in 1997 was inducted into the Rock and Roll Hall of Fame as a member of the Bee Gees. The Bee Gees received the award for Outstanding Contribution to Music at the 1997 Brit Awards. He was appointed a CBE (Commander of the British Empire) in 2002, receiving an honorary doctorate in 2004 from the University of Manchester in the UK.

Robin will be remembered as "one of the major figures in the history of British music... one of the best white soul voices ever" according to Paul Gambaccini.

MAURICE GIBB

Maurice Ernest Gibb, CBE, was born on the Isle of Man, United Kingdom on the 22nd of December 1949, just 30 minutes after his twin brother, Robin.

Music figured strongly in family life; father Hugh was a drummer and bandleader, but money was in short supply, so in 1958, when Maurice was 8 years old, the family moved to Australia.

With brothers Barry and Robin, Maurice had formed a band in the UK, and in their new home, the boys, singing three-part harmony with Maurice adding many of the higher ranges, rechristened themselves the Bee Gees. In Australia they had their first musical successes.

In 1966, Maurice took over as the lead guitarist and bassist for the band and also recorded 'All By Myself', his first solo composition, accompanying himself on guitar.

Now back in England, Maurice sang backing vocal harmony in the group, leaving the lead vocals to his brothers, but contributed as songwriter to many of the songs including their first No. 1 single in the UK, 'Massachusetts', which was released in September 1967.

When Robin left the band in 1969, Maurice and Barry continued as the Bee Gees for the album Cucumber Castle, on which Maurice wrote one song, 'My Thing' and co-wrote two others with Barry. A talented musician, Maurice's instrumental contribution was performed on bass guitar, acoustic guitar, piano and mellotron.

Maurice took to the high life, was friends with the Beatles, Michael Caine and David Bowie, and met the pop singer Lulu, who he married on the 18th February 1969; they divorced in 1975, forced apart by his heavy drinking.

Maurice released his first solo single, 'Railroad' in April 1970, and produced a solo album, Loner, which was never released.

Maurice was always known as a mild-mannered, stabilising influence, between his ambitious brothers, and once Robin was back on board after his rift with his brothers, the band enjoyed phenomenal success in the disco era.

Maurice and his second wife, Yvonne married, on the 17th of October 1975. They had two children, Adam and Samantha, and although he once pulled a gun on her, he curbed his drinking and they stayed together until his death.

Only 53 when he entered hospital for a twisted intestine, he died from a cardiac arrest shortly after.

Maurice was a skilled musician, and Barry Pethers said of him, "I owe him everything. His warmth and love will stay with me forever".

ANDY GIBB

Andrew Roy Gibb, CBE, was born in the Stretford Memorial Hospital, Manchester, England on March the 5th 1958.

Andy was just six months old and the youngest of five children born to Hugh and Barbara Gibb, when the family moved to Australia. Andy was the "little monkey with the heart of gold" of the family, who would skip school, eventually leaving at the age of 13 to play the guitar in Ibiza in Spain and later on the Isle of Man.

He formed his first group in 1974, Melody Fayre, managed by his mother. But at the suggestion of his brother Barry, he returned to Australia, releasing his first single, 'Words and Music', which became a top 20 hit in the Sydney chart in 1976. Andy married his girlfriend Kim Reeder that year, and they had a daughter, Peta; Andy and Kim divorced two years later.

Andy returned to England, and signed with Robert Stigwood's RSO records, Recording his first album, Flowing Rivers, for which Andy wrote 8 songs and which produced a No. 1 single in the United States and Australia,'I Just Want to be Your Everything'.

In 1978, Andy became the first male solo artist to have three consecutive No. 1 singles on the Billboard Hot 100; 'Shadow Dancing', 'Love is Thicker Than Water' and 'I Just Want to be Your Everything'.

Andy always doubted his ability to be a star in his own right, but often performed with his brothers. Andy, like his brothers, embraced the high life, and his drug abuse, which began in the 70s, started to affect his career and personal life. In the mid-80s he sought help at the Betty Ford Clinic, then managing to play music in small and large venues; but by 1987 he was compelled to enter another drug rehabilitation programme.

Barry tried to get him a record deal with Island Records in the UK, but he missed meetings and had difficulty writing songs and the deal fell through. Barry and the others then wanted to make him a fourth member of the Bee Gees.

Deeply depressed when Victoria Principal ended their relationship because of his drug-taking, he was later fired from TV and stage shows, and Robert Stigwood also found Andy too difficult to manage. In 1987 he was declared bankrupt.

By the new year of 1988, Andy thought that he had finally beaten the drugs and began work on a new album. His 30th birthday fell on March the 5th; two days later he was rushed to hospital with chest pains. By the 10th, the diagnosis was still not clear. But the myocarditis, an inflammation of the heart muscle that had been brought about by years of cocaine abuse, had fatally weakened his heart, and later that day he slipped into unconsciousness and died.

Andy was flown back to the US and buried at Forest Lawn in L.A.

Andy Gibb received two Grammy Awards nominations and a nomination for Favourite Pop/Rock America Artist at the 6th American Music Awards.

ROBERT STIGWOOD

Robert Colin Stigwood, was born in Port Pirie in Australia on the 16th of April 1934. Stigwood started out as a copywriter in an advertising agency, emigrating to England in 1955. En route, he worked in Turkey, living in a small hut.

Once in the UK, he worked in a boys' institute and a theatre before starting a theatrical agency. Combining manager and producer roles, fascinated by the wheeler-dealer aspect and the ease with which money could be made, his business quickly expanded; which was fortunate, because he was a big spender and eventually the receivers were called in.

Stigwood was also famously threatened by promoter Don Arden and put in fear of his life if he ever interfered with any of Arden's protégées.

Undaunted, Stigwood persevered and rebuilt his company, taking Cream with Eric Clapton on board in 1966.

In 1967, he joined forces with NEMS run by Brian Epstein, which raised him to the top of the industry. It was then that he signed the Bee Gees, and put a great deal of effort into successfully kickstarting their career in the UK. Stigwood left NEMS when Epstein died.

One year later he began theatre production, making musical history with Hair and Oh! Calcutta. By the 1970s, he was involved in TV production, too, although by that time, his fortunes were waning alongside the floundering Bee Gees and a drug-filled Eric Clapton.

Then came successful films of Tommy and Jesus Christ Superstar before the disco craze hit and his Saturday Night Fever and Grease films burst onto the scene.

He and the Bee Gees later parted company acrimoniously over royalty payments.

In his later years, Stigwood concentrated mainly on musical theatre.

Robert Stigwood died on the 4th of January 2016 at the age of 81 in London, England.

DISCOGRAPHY

ALBUMS

Bee Gees Sing and Play 14 Barry Gibb Songs	November 1965		
Spicks and Specks	November 1966		
Bee Gees' 1st	July 1967	8 UK	7 US
Horizontal	February 1968	16 UK	12 US
Idea	September 1968	4 UK	17 US
Odessa	March 1969	10 UK	20 US
Cucumber Castle	April 1970	57 UK	94 US
2 Years On	November 1970	33 UK	32 US
Trafalgar	September 1971		34 US
To Whom It May Concern	October 1972		35 US
Life in a Tin Can	January 1973		69 US
Mr. Natural	June 1974		178 US
Main Course	June 1975		14 US
Children of the World	September 1976		8 US
Spirits Having Flown	February 1979	1 UK	1 US
Living Eyes	October 1981	73 UK	41 US
E.S.P	September 1987	5 UK	96 US
One	April 1989	29 UK	68 US
High Civilisation	March 1991	24 UK	
Size Isn't Everything	September 1993	23 UK	153 US
Still Waters	March 1997	2 UK	11 US
This Is Where I Came in	April 2001	6 UK	16 US

SINGLES

1963

The Battle of the Blue and Grey / The Three Kisses of Love
Timber! / Take Hold of That Star

1964

Peace of Mind / Don't Say Goodbye
Claustrophobia / Could It Be
Turn Around, Look at Me / The Travels of Jamie McPheeters

1965

Every Day I Have to Cry / You Wouldn't Know
Wine and Women / Follow the Wind
I Was a Lover, Leader of Men / And the Children Laughing

1966

I Want Home / Cherry Red
Monday's Rain / All of My Life
Spicks and Specks / I Am the World

1967

Born a Man / Big Chance		
New York Mining Disaster 1941 / I Can't See Nobody	12 UK	14 US
To love Somebody / Close Another Door	41 UK	17 US
Holiday / Every Christian Lion-Hearted		
Man Will Show You	6 UK	16 US
Massachusetts / Barker of the UFO	1 UK	11 US
World / Sir Geoffrey Saved the World	9 UK	

1968

Words / Sinking Ships	8 UK	15 US
Jumbo / The Singer Sang His Song	25 UK	157 US
I've Gotta Get a Message to You / Kitty Can	1 UK	8 US

I Started a Joke / Kilburn Towers		6 US

1969

First of May / Lamplight	6 UK	37 US
Tomorrow Tomorrow / Sun in My Morning	23 UK	54 US
Don't Forget to Remember / The Lord	2 UK	73 US

1970

Let There Be Love / Really and Sincerely		
If Only I Had My Mind on Something Else / Sweetheart		91 US
I.O.I.O / Sweetheart	49 UK	94 US
Lonely days / Man for All Seasons	33 UK	3 US

1971

Melody Fair / In the Morning		
How Can You Mend a Broken Heart / Country Woman		1 US
When the Swallows Fly / Give Your Best		
In the Morning / To Love Somebody		
Don't Wanna Live Inside Myself / Walking Back to Waterloo		53 US

1972

My World / On Time	16 UK	16 US
Israel / Dearest		
Run to Me / Road to Alaska	9 UK	16 US
A Sea of Smiling Faces / Please Don't Turn Out the Lights		
Alive / Paper Mache, Cabbages and Kings		34 US

1973

Saw a New Morning / My Life Has Been a Song		94 US
Wouldn't I Be Someone Else / Elisa		

1974

Mr. Natural / It Doesn't Matter Much to Me		93 US
Throw a Penny / I Can't Let You Go		

Charade / Heavy Breathing		
1975		
Jive Talkin' / Winds of Change	5 UK	1 US
Nights on Broadway / Edge of the Universe		7 US
1976		
Fanny (Be Tender With My Love) / Country Lanes		12 US
You Should Be dancing / Subway	41 UK	3 US
Love So Right / You stepped Into My Life		
Boogie Child / Lovers		12 US
Children of the World / Boogie Child		
Edge of the Universe (Live) / Words (Live)		26 US
1977		
How Deep is Your Love / Can't Keep a Good Man Down (Live)	3 UK	1 US
More Than a Woman / Children of the World		
Stayin' Alive / If I can't Have You	4 UK	1 US
1978		
Night Fever / Down the Road (Live)	1 UK	1 US
Sgt. Pepper's Lonely Hearts Club Band / With a Little Help From My Friends		
Too Much Heaven / Rest Your Love on Me	3 UK	1 US
1979		
Tragedy / Until	1 UK	1 US
Love You Inside Out / I'm Satisfied	13 UK	1 US
Spirits (Having Flown) / Wind of Change	16 UK	
1981		
He's a Liar / He's a Liar (Instrumental)		30 US
Living Eyes / I Still Love You		45 US

1983

The Woman in You / Stayin' Alive		24 US
Someone Belonging to Someone / I Love You Too Much	49 UK	49 US

1987

You Win Again / Backtafunk	1 UK	75 US
E.S.P / Overnight	51 UK	

1988

Crazy for Your Love / You Win Again	79 UK	
Angela / You Win Again (Remix)		

1989

Ordinary Lives / Wing and a Prayer	54 UK	
One / Flesh and Blood	71 UK	7 US

1990

Bodyguard Will You Ever Let Me

1991

Secret Love / Party With No Name	5 UK	
When He's Gone / True Confessions		
The Only Love / You Win Again (Live)		
Happy Ever After / Evolution		

1993

Paying the Price of Love / My Destiny	23 UK	74 US
For Whom the Bell Tolls / Decadance (You Should Be Dancing)	4 UK	

1994

How to Fall in Love. Part 1 / Fallen Angel	30 UK	
Kiss of Life / 855-7019		

1995			
Will You Love Me Tomorrow			
1997			
Alone / Rings Around the Moon		5 UK	28 US
I Could Not Love You More / Love Never Dies			14 UK
Still Waters (Run Deep) / Love Never Dies		18 UK	57 US
1998			
Immortality (With Celine Dion) / My Heart Will Go On		5 UK	
2000			
This is Where I came In / Just in Case/I Will Be There		18 UK	

LIVE ALBUMS

Here at Last... Bee Gees... Live	May 1977		8 US
One Night Only	Sept 1998	4 UK	72 US

SOUNDTRACKS

Melody (Bee Gees and various artists)	May 1971		
Saturday Night Fever (Bee Gees and various artists)	Nov 1977	1 UK	1 US
Sgt. Pepper's Lonely Hearts Club Band (various artists)	July 1978	38 UK	5 US
Staying Alive (Bee Gees and various artists)	June 1983	14 UK	6 US